Vanished Villages of
ELGIN

Vanished Villages of

ELGIN

Jennifer Grainger

NATURAL HERITAGE BOOKS
A MEMBER OF THE DUNDURN GROUP
TORONTO

Published by Natural Heritage Books
A Member of The Dundurn Group
3 Church Street, Suite 500
Toronto, Ontario, M5E 1M2, Canada
www.dundurn.com

Library and Archives Canada Cataloguing in Publication

Grainger, Jennifer
  Vanished villages of Elgin / Jennifer Grainger.

Includes bibliographical references and index.
ISBN 978-1-55002-812-6

  1. Elgin (Ont. : County)--History. I. Title.

FC3095.E44Z58 2008   971.3'25   C2008-900236-9

1   2   3   4   5   12   11   10   09   08

Front Cover: top left, Mill stones, Springwater Conservation Area; right, Monument to the Talbot Settlement; bottom, the Harding Mill at Selbourne, early 1900s, *courtesy of Elgin County Archives C3Sb6B1F18.*
Back Cover: top right, a postcard shows the harbour at Port Bruce, c. 1909, *courtesy of Elgin County Archives C6Sb6B4F1#39*; bottom left, Campbellton General Store and Post Office, c. 1900, *courtesy of Archives of Ontario F2178-1-0-17.*

All photos in the text were taken by the author unless otherwise credited.

Cover design by Erin Mallory
Text design by Jennifer Scott
Edited by Jane Gibson
Copyedited by John Parry
Printed and bound in Canada by Transcontinental

Care has been taken to trace the ownership of copyright material used in this book. The author and the publisher welcome any information enabling them to rectify any references or credits in subsequent editions.

J. Kirk Howard, President

Conseil des Arts du Canada   Canada Council for the Arts   Canada   ONTARIO ARTS COUNCIL   CONSEIL DES ARTS DE L'ONTARIO

We acknowledge the support of the **Canada Council for the Arts** and the **Ontario Arts Council** for our publishing program. We also acknowledge the financial support of the **Government of Canada** through the **Book Publishing Industry Development Program** and **The Association for the Export of Canadian Books** and the **Government of Canada** through the **Ontario Book Publishers Tax Credit Program** and the **Ontario Media Development Corporation**.

Dundurn Press	Gazelle Book Services Limited	Dundurn Press
3 Church Street, Suite 500	White Cross Mills	2250 Military Road
Toronto, Ontario, Canada	High Town, Lancaster, England	Tonawanda, NY
M5E 1M2	LA1 4XS	U.S.A. 14150

CONTENTS

Acknowledgements

When I research a book, I am always grateful to the many people who assist me along the way. This volume could not have been written without the help of the staff at the London Room at the Central Public Library in London, the George Thorman Room at the St. Thomas Public Library, the Elgin County Archives, the Archives of Ontario, and the Archives and Research Collections Centre, University of Western Ontario. Many thanks also to Catherine Elliot Shaw of the McIntosh Gallery at Western for her assistance in providing the copy of the portrait of Colonel Thomas Talbot, and to Mike Baker of the Elgin County Museum for help with the picture of Colonel Mahlon Burwell.

Many other people provided me with stories and photos for this book: Lee and Audrey Ball (Griffin's or Froggett's Corners), Don Carroll (Campbellton and Largie), Margaret Carroll (Middlemarch), Richard and Mona Cline (West Magdala), Tony Csinos (Estherville), Glen Curnoe (Selbourne), Josephine Froggett (Griffin's or Froggett's Corners), Jean Griffin (Dexter), Evelina Hartemink (Crossley-Hunter), Ruth Howard (Crinan), Harley and Nancy Lashbrook (Aldborough Township communities), Minnie Livingstone (Crinan), Ruby McGugan (Coyne's Corners), John McIntyre (Crinan), Duncan McKillop (Killerby), Catherine McMillan (Kintyre), Norman McWilliam (Campbellton), Kathleen Oatman (Glencolin), Norma Schneckenburger (Churchville), Harris

Teall (Griffin's Corners), William Vanidour (Pleasant Valley), and Barbara and Al Willey (Churchville).

Finally, thanks to my parents, Bob and Norma Grainger, for moral support and 'photo expeditions.'

Of course, while every effort has been made to ensure accuracy of information throughout, the responsibility for any errors rests with me.

INTRODUCTION

THE SUCCESS OF *Vanished Villages of Middlesex* has prompted me to write about vanished villages in Elgin. Just like Middlesex, Elgin County had many small communities scattered across its landscape, and just as in Middlesex, many have faded away.

The typical crossroads hamlets of nineteenth-century Elgin included a general store and post office, blacksmith, church, and school. There might also have been a mill or two, carriage-making shop, hotel, and shoemaker. In the days when most of our population was rural, small villages such as these were important centres of support for the scattered homesteads. Roads were poor, and travel by horse and buggy was slow. Pioneers couldn't travel far to buy their groceries, mail a letter, have a horse shod, worship, or send their children to school. These hamlets were also places where neighbours could meet to chat about the weather, discuss politics, or just have a friendly gossip.

Several factors contributed to the disappearance of these tiny communities. One was the general trend towards urban living over the last century and a half. Young people moved to the city to attend school and find work, and farming became not as common an occupation as in times past. A second factor was the building of the railways, which contributed to the growth of some villages and the decline of others as businesses would shift location, abandoning one place if necessary in order to be close to the rail lines. A third factor was the rise of the automobile, which led to faster travel on better roads and lessened the need for so many small service centres. In some cases, natural disasters such as floods and economic downturns caused by the decline of certain industries such as lumbering contributed to the demise of many of Elgin's villages. Also, just as the city of London absorbed many surrounding villages through annexation over the years, Elgin's county seat, St. Thomas, acquired one of its neighbouring centres.

Elgin County was originally part of the Western District of (Upper) Canada, which was divided in 1792 into four counties — Norfolk, Suffolk, Essex, and Kent. Bayham, Malahide, and South Dorchester townships were initially part of Norfolk County, while Yarmouth, Southwold, Dunwich, and Aldborough townships were in Suffolk County. It was Lieutenant-Governor John Graves Simcoe and his staff who named many of the townships, several of them after towns in Suffolk (county), England. The idea seems to have been to reproduce the geography of England as much as possible in Upper Canada. Suffolk County was short-lived, however, as was the Western District. In 1798 the Western District was partitioned into several new territories, including the London District, which was composed of the counties of Norfolk, Middlesex, and Oxford. Today this land mass is divided into Elgin, Middlesex, Oxford, Norfolk, Huron, and Bruce counties. The county of Middlesex consisted of the townships of London, Westminster, Dorchester, Delaware, Yarmouth, Southwold, Dunwich, and Aldborough. It was not until 1837 that the townships of Bayham and Malahide became part of Middlesex. Finally, in August 1851, the Territorial Division Act created Elgin County as we know it today. Dorchester Township was at that time split into north and south, and the southern section was transferred to Elgin. St. Thomas was chosen as the county seat because of its central location.[1]

The name of this new county derived from the title of James Bruce, eighth Earl of Elgin (1811–1863), governor general of Canada from 1847 to 1854. His title came from the community of Elgin in Moray, Scotland. Lord Elgin had visited Port Stanley in 1850,[2] his presence possibly contributing to a local desire to name the new county after him. Colonel Thomas Talbot had campaigned unsuccessfully to have the new county named after himself.[3]

A county is a convenient unit to use when doing a study of local history. From a geographic perspective, Elgin is smaller than

Middlesex. Beyond size, there are other differences between the two adjacent counties. Elgin is on Lake Erie and consequently, though newer, began developing earlier. The earliest pioneers first settled along the shores of the lake before penetrating farther inland.

Many of Elgin's original settlers were United Empire Loyalists, fleeing the American Revolutionary War. As well, the War of 1812 played a far more important role in Elgin's history than in that of Middlesex since it was closer to the United States border and often under attack. Being on the lake meant Elgin developed many lake ports, some of which have disappeared. Also, unlike Middlesex, Elgin's history is dominated by the legend of one man — Colonel Thomas Talbot — whose early influence was extraordinary.

I found doing research on Elgin's past in many ways easier than exploring Middlesex's history. In general, Elgin has done a better job of preserving its heritage, even possessing a county archives. Another trend of the last decade, since my earlier work on Middlesex, has been the increased amount of historical information on the internet.

Thanks also to the excellent websites of organizations such as the Elgin County Archives and the Elgin Branch of the Ontario Genealogical Society, it has been possible for me to spend many evenings researching vanished villages in Elgin from the comfort of my own home! Yet in the past ten years an older generation of former residents has passed away, and fewer people have memories to assist me. Many of the small villages of Elgin seem now to be just beyond human recollection.

As I did with *Vanished Villages of Middlesex*, I have divided this book into the historic nineteenth-century townships that the early settlers would have recognized. I present a short description of each to acquaint readers with its history and character and a map to show the location of the various places. Many communities on old maps of Elgin were not true villages or even hamlets but often only a post office, church, school, or farm, usually at a crossroads. Sometimes I mention these names in passing, but I reserve the larger stories for "real" communities.

More has been written about some communities and townships than others. This difference reflects the nature of the records. Historians wrote a great deal about Port Talbot and Tyrconnell, for example, because they are in one of the earliest settled parts of southwestern Ontario, in the heart of the Talbot Settlement. There is probably as much information about these two communities in Dunwich Township as about the rest of the county combined. Other townships and their settlements have received less coverage. Writings on Bayham Township in particular seem scarce; I often have had to rely on its residents' memories to supplement my research.

Courtesy of Elgin County Archives R6S5Sb1B2F29

The Talbot home, c. 1993, just before it was torn down.

As in Middlesex, the need for more heritage conservation in Elgin is obvious. We have lost many pioneer cabins, country churches, one-room schoolhouses, railway depots, stores, and factories — all historic, many unique — that might have been adapted to other purposes. The most obvious example has been the demolition of the Port Talbot residence of Colonel Talbot himself — Malahide. With dedicated restoration, Talbot's old pioneer home could have become a tourist attraction, a museum to commemorate the Talbot Settlement where Elgin County began.

I hope this book will be useful to readers who wish to understand more about the many once-vibrant but now vanished villages of Elgin and that it will bring particular pleasure to those with roots in these communities. I would also like to think that many will take the opportunity to explore the countryside of Elgin with this volume in hand and rediscover the richness of that which has gone before.

CHAPTER ONE

TOWNSHIP OF ALDBOROUGH

ELGIN'S WESTERNMOST HISTORICAL township was formed in 1792 as part of what was originally Suffolk County. It was named after a seacoast town in Suffolk, England, formerly spelled as Aldborough but today usually written as Aldeburgh. The name means "old borough," a borough being a fortified place.[1] In medieval times the English town developed into a prosperous fishing and shipbuilding port and was the birthplace of English poet George Crabbe (1754–1832), whose poems *The Village* (1783) and *The Borough* (1810) described the harsh lives of working people in Aldborough. It has been suggested that Lieutenant-Governor John Graves Simcoe and his staff may have chosen the name because Crabbe's poetry appealed to them.[2] Most of the early settlers of nineteenth-century Aldborough Township were immigrants from Scotland or Germany.

In January 1998, Aldborough and the villages of West Lorne and Rodney were united to form the municipality of West Elgin.

Churchville

Churchville, at the corner of Kerr Road and Middle Street (now Thomson Line), was the centre of a German settlement in the nineteenth century. At one time, it had three churches and three cemeteries.

About 1840, Germans of Lutheran, Evangelical, and Roman Catholic faiths started settling in Aldborough Township, emigrating

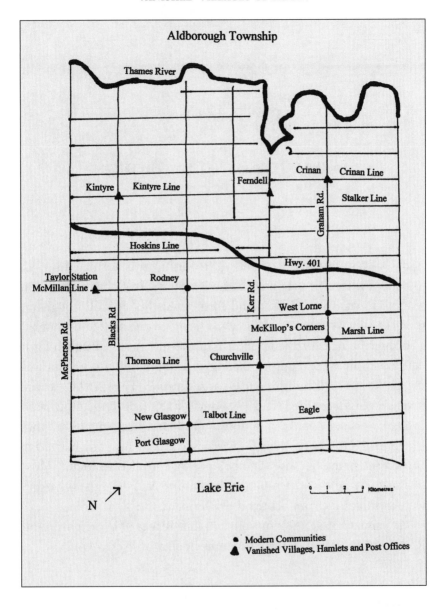

Aldborough Township

Thames River

Kintyre Kintyre Line Ferndell Crinan Crinan Line

Graham Rd. Stalker Line

Hoskins Line

Hwy. 401

Taylor Station Rodney Kerr Rd.
McMillan Line West Lorne

McPherson Rd. Blacks Rd. McKillop's Corners Marsh Line

Thomson Line Churchville

New Glasgow Talbot Line Eagle

Port Glasgow

Lake Erie

N

• Modern Communities
▲ Vanished Villages, Hamlets and Post Offices

to North America usually by way of the United States. By 1877, it was estimated that one-tenth of the population of the township was of German descent.[3] Not surprisingly, Page's *Illustrated Historical Atlas of the County of Elgin* that year has a listing on its frontspiece of various buildings, such as "farmhouse," "school," and "church," translated into German. It was some time before many of these settlers could acquire facility in the English language.

In 1860, Henry Sauer began holding services for those of the Evangelical faith. He walked all the way from the Fort Erie area to what became Churchville and held services in various homes until the Canada Company[4] granted land for a place of worship in 1861. Solomon McColl of Brock's Creek (now Eagle) and Adam Baker built the original Emanuel Evangelical Church. When a new frame structure was constructed in 1876 by J.J. Mistele for $1,690,[5] the first building became a storage shed. Although the congregation founded its cemetery west of the intersection in 1875, the church itself was on the northeast corner. A manse for the German-speaking minister went up right behind the church. It would be 1920 before worship or any form of services took place in English.

In the 1850s, two couples, Henry and Regina and Wendelin and Josepha, both with the surname Schneckenburger, arrived at the intersection with their families. Other German Catholics followed them, and in 1858 some Irish families. Priests came once a year from Chatham on horseback and said mass in the home of Henry and Regina. Often Regina would act as the interpreter in confession for some elderly Germans who could not speak English.

In the autumn of 1866, disaster struck. Henry went to plough a garden for a neighbour; as he was leaving, a dog frightened his

St. Henry's Roman Catholic, the last remaining place of worship at Churchville, is boarded up.

horses, causing them to bolt and lurch against a small stump. The impact was enough to throw the heavy wooden plough back, injuring Henry so seriously that he lived only for another six months. The nearest Catholic cemetery was at Wardsville, but the combination of bad weather and poor roads led Regina to decide to donate land for a cemetery and church on her farm.[6]

But first it was necessary to raise the funds. W. Flannery, the parish priest in St. Thomas in the 1870s, visited the area and went about collecting subscriptions from local Catholics. Feeling he was not doing well enough, he then went out another day and approached local Protestants, so the story goes. On the following Sunday, he read a mass in one of the Catholic homes and in front of the congregation counted the contributions he had received. The Protestants had given more, making their contributions the greater. He concluded: "What am I to build — a Protestant or a Catholic church?" There was an immediate increase in Catholic subscriptions.[7]

Accordingly, in 1870, the first Catholic church in Elgin County[8] was built on the south side of Middle Street just west of Kerr Road. The cost of construction for the structure, standing 22 feet by 30 feet, was $450.[9] Regina and her sister-in-law Josepha went to Buffalo to purchase the altar and statues, which they had shipped to Newbury, Middlesex County, and then had Regina's sons Joseph, John, and Henry transport them to the site. The church was named St. Henry's after Regina's late husband. Years later, in 1922, William Schneckenburger built an archway to the grounds with Robert Schneckenburger of Buffalo donating the $350 for it.[10]

St. Peter's Evangelical Lutheran Church was the next to appear, south of Middle Street on the east side of Kerr Road. It was built sometime between 1864 and 1874 on land donated by the Canada Company. The Schleihauf family, whose members represent most of the burials there, donated a plaque on the cemetery gate. This is the final resting place of Otto Bismark Schleihauf (see McKillop's Corners, Bismarck, and Lorne).

Because of the three churches all around the intersection, local resident Philip Schmeltz named the settlement Churchville.[11] But there were a few enterprising businesses nearby as well. At some point, Wendelin Schneckenburger's brick factory sat on the southeast

The rebuilt church as it looks today.

Presbyterian congregations in 1925 — Argyle decided to remain Presbyterian and linked with Duff's Church in Largie. Argyle Church was rebuilt in the 1940s when the floor was sagging and the foundation had settled. With all able-bodied men in the congregation assisting, and by using materials from the old church in the new one, it was possible to keep costs down and reopen Argyle on Sunday, June 17, 1948. The new building was shifted twenty feet back from the roadway.

Crinan received its name when Duncan McIntyre arrived. He set up a small store and tailor shop near the school in the 1850s and made suits from durable wool, carded, spun into yarn, and woven into cloth by local women with looms. Soon he decided to go into the mail business as well, and Crinan post office opened June 1, 1859, in his shop.[14] The name was chosen not by McIntyre but by local resident Peter McNeil, who had put forward the name of his hometown in Argyle, Scotland. Crinan is also the name of a Scottish loch and canal. This moniker attached itself to the school, the church when it was built, and the entire community; in Canada it is pronounced "Creenan."

At first, mail came once a week from Wardsville in Middlesex County. Delivery involved crossing the river on the scow mentioned above — a dubious mode of transportation consisting of three canoes attached together and covered with planks. A Mr. Sutton kept it on his farm on the south bank of the river. This routing continued until the Canada Southern Railroad built its tracks through Dutton in 1872, making it possible to bring in mail three times a week from Dutton. The scow continued to be used by folks doing business in Wardsville until 1876, when a wooden bridge was erected over the river, supported jointly by both Elgin and Middlesex counties.

There was an attempt to construct a replacement in iron over the Thames in 1888, but disaster struck. When the span was almost completed, it gave way and collapsed. Dan Mitchell, who was standing on it at the time, felt the structure shake and leaped into the river in time to save his life. Others were not so fortunate. A Mr. Lamb was thrown into the water and drowned. Mr. G. Weekes, a blacksmith at Woodgreen, Mosa Township, heard the commotion, harnessed his horse, and rushed to the river. On the way he met Mitchell, who was hurrying home in wet clothes to get assistance. Despite the loss of life, workmen eventually resumed work. Materials were salvaged from the river, and construction began anew.[15]

Meanwhile, back at Crinan, other businesses were emerging. A few years after McIntyre's business opened, in 1869 Robert McMillan built a cheese factory opposite the church. The Markham family came from Ingersoll to manage the factory, bringing along a herd of purebred Holstein cattle. Thomas Markham bought the business in 1909. At first, the Markhams gathered milk from farmers' milk stands at the end of their laneways. Later each farmer delivered his own milk and could refill his cans with whey held in a tank beside the factory. Hog farmers were especially pleased to get this whey for pig feed.

There were two other cheesemakers in the area, a Mr. Thompson and a Clarence Beckett. There is also a reference to the Crinan Cheese Factory opening in April 1884,[16] so either there were two cheese factories in the neighbourhood or the original factory closed and was later reopened.

It is not known what became of McIntyre's store. However, cheesemaker Thomas Markham built a store of his own to the south of his cheese factory. It carried groceries, clothing, hardware, and coal oil. It also had a barber's chair where Dick or David Markham cut hair.

This store was later run by the enterprise of Wrights, Brydens, and Cooks. Frequently, community dances and oyster suppers were held in a hall upstairs. The village also had a blacksmith shop kept by A. Young and a shoemaking shop kept by either Donald Young or Donald McCall. The first phone line between West Lorne and Glencoe was built in 1900, running right through Crinan. The "central" was at the Crinan post office, and Jessie McIntyre was operator. It is estimated that the population of the area about this time might have been roughly fifty people.

A dance hall known as "the bunkhouse," "the summer kitchen," "the boxing ring," and sometimes just "the hall," was a popular feature in the 1930s. It was originally a Sunday school building from miles away, purchased by a Mr. McAlpine about 1930. One February, it was moved on sleighs pulled by four teams of horses. McAlpine intended to add the new building to his house so there would be more room for his family, but as the Depression was in full swing he found he had not enough money to make the needed renovations. Instead it sat on blocks, unused. Once some creative person suggested it would be a good place to hold a square dance, the building gained a new lease on life. The McPherson family provided music for the first of many dances. Dave McPherson was the caller, announcing the next dance with "Fill up the floor!" The events were so popular that they were held every second Friday in winter throughout the Depression. Admission was a lunch dish from the women and 25¢ from the men. For years the season would open in the autumn with a Hallowe'en party conducted by the Women's Institute. In summer the building became a bunkhouse for boys and hired men and a good place to practise wrestling.

Of course, in a staunchly Presbyterian neighbourhood, not everyone approved of such activities as dances. Grandfather McAlpine, who lived in Dutton, disapproved of these activities, but his son persuaded him to come to a dance. Before long the old man was performing a Scottish reel, and on leaving he inquired, "When are you going to have the next one?"[17]

Gradually, in the twentieth century, buildings disappeared. The last operator of the store was Charles Cook in 1923. Malcolm Livingstone bought the property, sold the building, and had it torn down in 1928. The Markham cheese factory ran into difficulties when the Markhams installed a large cream separator. Since the whey put through it was no longer available for pigs, dissatisfaction grew among the farmers. They tried running the factory for a while themselves as a co-operative, but they began to distrust one another and all operations ceased. The last operator was Clarence Beckett, and the factory closed about 1916. In the early 1930s, its buildings were sold and the facility became a barn. The building in which the whey vat was kept became a garage for the Livingstone family. The dance hall closed during the Second World War when the young men went off to serve in the war effort. The last party there was in the 1940s. The school closed in 1965 and was sold to a Mr. Haddish of Rodney.[18] The building burned in the 1970s.

Crinan post office survived longer than some other businesses. When its founder, Duncan McIntyre, died, his son John succeeded him as postmaster and moved the office to a building on his farm on the north side of the road, east of the intersection. John ran the post office until his death in 1916, after which Jessie McIntyre took over and continued it until her own death in 1942. Edna and Stewart McIntyre were the next to take it over and kept it in a corner of their kitchen. Finally, on July 1, 1967, government officials came and picked up three sets of scales and other equipment; Crinan post office became part of RR 1, West Lorne. The McIntyre family had operated the facility for 108 years.

Argyle Presbyterian Church remains on the northeast corner of the intersection and is still holding services. Recently the size of its congregation increased when West Lorne Knox Presbyterian closed in 1998 and several of its members started attending church in Crinan. Across the street on the Livingstone property is an old well that marks the site of the store and cheese factory. The third house, to the east of the intersection on the north side, was the McIntyre residence, and the small building near the road was the post office. The Crinan Women's Institute Community Centre has commemorated the name of the village at the southeast corner of Duff Line and Dunborough Road.

This little roadside cabin was once the Crinan post office.

The name "Crinan" is preserved in the Community Centre at Duff Line and Dunborough Road.

Ferndell

A schoolhouse was built at the corner of Division Line (now Colley Road) and Stalker Line in 1888. Mrs. William Haines, wife of the oldest trustee, named it Fern Dell after the large number of ferns growing in the area.[19] In time, the two words were compressed, creating Ferndell as the popular name for the settlement. The school, after serving as a centre for the community for many years, was closed in 1965, and the building demolished.

An item in the *Dutton Advance* on December 4, 1890, from the Fern Dell correspondent states, "Our burg is growing. We have two saw mills. We want a post-office, store, church and blacksmith shop yet." The article reports that a Mr. H. McDonald had moved his portable sawmill to Ferndell and was planning to start sawing soon. There is no indication the intersection ever acquired the other buildings.

Kintyre

Kintyre consisted of a church, school, and post office. Knox Church Kintyre was built on the southeast corner of Concession 4 (now Kintyre Line) and Black's Lane (now Black's Road) and still stands there today. To the south, on the northwest corner of Hoskins Line and Black's Lane, was SS No. 7 Aldborough, known locally as Fleming School.

The Kintyre post office was located in a house on the northeast corner of the southern intersection although at one point it was within

Stained glass above the doorway of Kintyre Church spells out the name of the former post office.

the school itself. Mail came daily from Taylor Station. The post office opened on September 1, 1894, under James Fleming and closed on May 13, 1913, when Sarah Brodie was postmaster. According to Sarah's daughter Catherine McMillan, this house was just recently demolished in a controlled burn.[20]

McKillop's Corners, Bismarck, and Lorne

The village of West Lorne was not always as it appears today. It began one intersection to the south, under the name of McKillop's Corners, and developed at its present location in two sections. The three small communities of McKillop's Corners, Bismarck, and Lorne have all merged into West Lorne.

McKillop's Corners developed at the corner of Graham Road and Hog Street (now Marsh Line). It seems that Hog Street, sometimes spelled "Hogg" in an attempt to add distinction, received its name because some early settlers kept pigs.[21] However, it was also known as Mill Street, as there were a number of early mills located along its way.

For some unknown reason the community was sometimes referred to as "Poemsville;" no explanation could be found in any source. McKillop's Corners was certainly more appropriate, since that family founded the village. Archibald McKillop started a sawmill business on a northern branch of Brock's Creek about 1856 in order to harvest the hardwood timber, such as chestnut, that once covered this area. Trees four and five feet in diameter were cut into boards. The lumber was then transported by wagon down to Eagle, a village on Lake Erie, and shipped over the lake to Buffalo. Archibald's sons, Archibald Jr. and Duncan, joined him in the business, and the family eventually had a gristmill and planing mill in operation as well.

The village, consisting of a general store, blacksmith shop, cheese factory, church, school, and some houses, developed around this mill complex. The school was the earliest of all these buildings, the first structure having been built between 1825 and 1830. The fee to attend, before free education arrived, was two-and-a-half bushels of wheat per pupil. An extra bushel purchased a spelling book.[22] John Peates, the first teacher, boarded at the homes of various pupils for one week at a time. Later, a frame building went up on the west side of the road north of the intersection in the 1860s or 1870s. A Methodist church was constructed on a farm belonging to William Clark and was part of the same charge as Tyrconnell. There were also Baptists in the neighbourhood; records indicate that they performed their baptisms in McKillop's millpond. By the 1880s, on Hogg (or Mill) Street, a co-operative cheese factory began; it would continue operating for many years with John McDiarmid as president and John F. Taylor as secretary-treasurer.

The Canada Southern Railway[23] built a line north of this intersection in 1871–72. There were only about two houses near the tracks, but before long it became obvious that a location by the railway tracks was the ideal place. McKillop's Corners did not develop further, and business and industry started gathering around the tracks. Once the rail line was operating, it was more economical for the McKillops to use it to ship their hardwood. From then on, hundreds of cords of wood were shipped annually by train.[24] Eventually, in 1884, the McKillops decided to relocate their business to the very edge of the tracks themselves.

The new community developed so rapidly that by 1877 there were four hundred to five hundred people, with five stores, three hotels, and two churches noted in the records.[25] Duncan McKillop owned a large gristmill and stave factory, Archibald McKillop had a sawmill, and John C. Schleihauf ran a saw and shingle mill, in addition to a lath and planing mill. By 1886 the population had grown to eight hundred people.[26]

In 1853, John Schleihauf settled on Mill Street where he also located his mills. By 1860, he had also purchased land at what became northern West Lorne. A few years later, in 1872, he donated seventeen acres of land to the Canada Southern Railway for the building of a station, on the condition that the line name it Bismarck, after the German chancellor.[27] In another indicator of Schleihauf's admiration for the statesman, he and his wife, Sarah, also named one of their children Otto Bismark[28] (see Churchville).

The McKillops, however, had their own ideas about what the new community should be called. Their family business was Lorne

Mills. They may have chosen this name after John, Marquis of Lorne, governor general of Canada 1878–83, husband of Princess Louise, Queen Victoria's daughter. The McKillops originated from the part of Scotland whence the marquis took his title — Argyle, just east of the Firth of Lorne. The Lornes never visited West Lorne, but they did get as close as St. Thomas, and many of the Highlanders in the county went, hoping to see them.

It has been said that the Celtic meaning for Lorne is "low and swampy."[29] This name is appropriate, since the Canadian location was swampy as well. However, it may mean "territory of Loarn's tribe," after Loarn Mar, "the great fox," who lived about the year 500.[30]

Prior to the coming of the railway, mail was carried by horseback from Eagle and left at the home of Duncan McKillop, the area's first postmaster. An official post office opened January 1, 1873, prompted no doubt by the arrival of the rail line. The first name was West Clayton, but as Clayton was also a post office in Lanark County, confusion resulted. On February 1, the name was changed to Dutton but this too was short-lived. And on July 1 it was altered to West Lorne, which it remains. It is not known what "west" refers to — west of Scotland? In all likelihood, Duncan McKillop picked the final moniker to honour his family business. He kept the office in a white frame building on the northeast corner of Graham and Main streets (the main intersection) and lived upstairs. West Lorne's longest-serving postmaster, he kept his position until he passed away on July 4, 1919.

So it came about that both the village on the north side of the tracks and the station were called Bismarck, and the village on the south side of the tracks was Lorne, while the post office was called West Lorne. Archibald McKillop suggested to his rival, John Schleihauf, that they come up with a compromise by dropping both names and choosing a new one on which they could both agree — but to no avail. Schleihauf wanted "Bismarck." The situation remained this way for quite some time. Page's *Illustrated Historical Atlas of the County of Elgin* for 1877 shows two distinct villages — Bismark and Lorne. When trains went through, the conductor would announce the next stop with "Bismarck Station, West Lorne."[31]

Eventually the railway itself brought an end to this situation. There was another Bismarck in the Niagara area near Grimsby. When

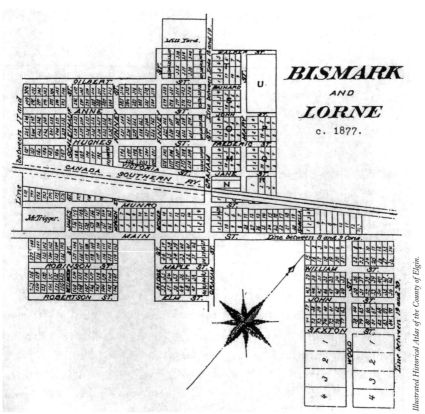

This 1877 map shows the locations of the community of Bismarck north of the Canada Southern Railway and the village of Lorne south of the line. It would be many years before the two combined to form West Lorne.

W.S. Morden's business was in Bismarck, on the north side of the tracks at West Lorne.

a carload of freight went to the wrong Bismarck and was unloaded there while the railway company endeavored in vain to trace its whereabouts,[32] the Michigan Central Railroad[33] made the decision. The name Bismarck was dropped from its station at West Lorne in 1907. Schleihauf started a lawsuit over it, but there was much anti-German feeling in Canada during the build-up to the First World War and Schleihauf's protest was not heeded. He died shortly thereafter, in 1908, and his family, perhaps wisely, did not pursue the matter. West Lorne was incorporated as a village on December 21, 1907.

Today West Lorne has about 1,400 people and stretches out to the original location of McKillop's Corners. The railway tracks were ripped up a few years ago, and Bismarck Station is long gone.

Taylor Station

A set of rail tracks once passed over McMillan Line, between Black's and McPherson roads. This was the site of Taylor Station, one of the busiest railway stops between Windsor and St. Thomas.

The Canada Southern Railway bought one hundred acres there, as the location could provide a source of water for its locomotives and gravel for its roadbeds, and laid its tracks through in 1871–72. They built a well, pump house, water tank, and, of course, station. The little facility was only 24 feet by 40 feet, but four passenger trains, two in each direction, stopped there daily. Mail for Kintyre post office (see Kintyre) was dropped off daily, and outgoing mail was picked up and sorted in mail cars. A telegrapher was on duty around the clock, and two section gangs worked out of Taylor because of the continual repair required on the single line. In the early days there were frequent derailments because of the rails' tendency to spread and shift.

Two stave mills were also located near the tracks — one owned by a D. Waugh and one by a R. Whitehead. Horse-drawn wagons and sleighs brought elm logs to the mills, where they were cut into barrel-length staves and sent by train to Detroit and Buffalo. Others went by wagon to Port Glasgow, a village on Lake Erie, to be shipped to American ports on the south side of the lake. Two spur lines were built from the station – one south of the main line to the mills, and the other north, for loading cordwood and gravel.

Because of growing rail traffic, both passenger and freight, the demand for water soon exceeded the capacity of the railway's well near the station. To provide another source of water, the Canada Southern dug what became known as Taylor Pond, 200 feet wide, 400 feet long, and 10 feet deep. It then installed water tanks so passenger trains could retrieve water quickly while going by. The engineer dropped a scoop into the tank, and the speed of the train forced water into the tender — enough to last until the next stop in St. Thomas or Windsor.

Clay from the pond was used to form a base for the second rail line that was added later. The Pere Marquette Railroad laid out its line 100 feet to the south and built a station on the south side of the tracks, 12 feet by 18 feet, about 2,000 feet from its competitor. [34] The Pere Marquette offered east- and west-bound passenger service daily, with most travellers going to Ridgetown, Blenheim, and Chatham. The station had a stove, windows, and a door that no one ever locked. At night it became a euchre den for area farmers, and in cold weather vagrants slept there for the warmth of the stove. [35]

With all this activity going on, a small village soon developed around the tracks. By the late nineteenth century, it had a general store and more than a dozen houses. Yet it was not to last. Michigan Central took over the Canada Southern in 1882, and in 1904 the Pere Marquette secured running rights over the tracks. In the 1920s, the New York Central [36] made a business decision that led to Taylor's demise. The rail company moved the track tanks to West Lorne, where hydro was available. A new station was built at Muirkirk in Kent County, and afterwards the village of Taylor started to die.

Taylor Pond gained new use as a recreational facility. The New York Central stocked it with green bass, but few locals were interested in fishing. Instead, the pond became the local swimming hole. On a warm Sunday afternoon in the early twentieth century, as many as eighty-five young men would be there. Eventually they organized themselves into softball teams and played in the area around the pond. Teenage boys would hop on board a Pere Marquette freight car while it

All that remains of Taylor Station: the beds of the former railway lines and a few scattered hydro poles among the weeds.

was on the siding west of Rodney, and when the train was going slowly at Taylor they would jump off and go swim at the pond. Section men returning from the west would generally stop to pick them up and take them on a fast ride back to the village at the end of the day. Unfortunately, not all was idyllic. Two young men once drowned while trying to swim the 200 feet across the pond. One was a teller at Rodney's Royal Bank.[37]

Today, the area is quiet. Even the railway tracks have been removed in the last couple of years. The only reminders of the former stations are the railway beds and a few hydro poles where the tracks once were. The pond still exists among a cluster of trees but is now on private property.

Chapter Two

Township of Bayham

Surveyed in 1810, Elgin's easternmost township was named after Charles Pratt, Earl Camden, and Viscount Bayham (1714–94). His title came from the ruins of Bayham Abbey, Kent, built in 1200, and owned by his family.[1] Viscount Bayham was a friend of Colonel Thomas Talbot's, who probably named the township after him.[2] The ancestral background of most of the early settlers was English, with a few Scots mixed in. However, some pioneers moved here from Digby County, Nova Scotia, about the time of the War of 1812, which is why there is Nova Scotia Line near the lakeshore. In January 1998, Bayham Township united with the villages of Vienna and Port Burwell to form the municipality of Bayham.

Estherville

The precursor to Port Burwell would have been found near the corner of Plank Road and Concession 1 Bayham (now Glen Erie Line) on Otter Creek. The site was first settled by Joseph Merrill, who built a road and bridge over the stream. Anyone travelling through the area would have had to go through the community first known as Merrill's Corners.

As it was on a creek that emptied into Lake Erie, by the 1830s the area had developed into a shipyard. Many settlers were from Nova Scotia and were adept at building and sailing small schooners. The oak and hard maple that grew nearby made it a natural location

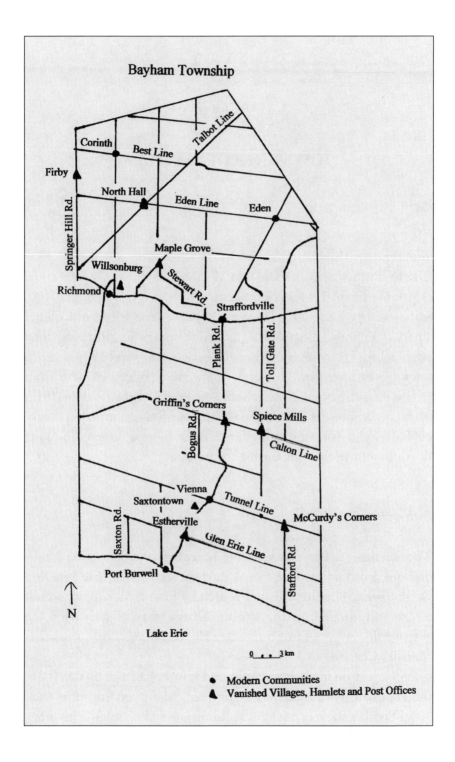

for a shipyard. The oak actually grew on the slopes of the valley in the shape of the bends and ribs of a ship's hull. The long planks used in the hull sheaving were brought down by barge from sawmills on the Big Otter. They were then steamed and shaped in the shipyard.[3] Several stores as well as a hotel were built in the community.

Thomas Hollowood, who owned property nearby, may have changed the name from Merrill's Corners to Estherville after his wife, Esther. They may not have had a loving marriage, however, since "they had earlier been to court over marital difficulties and were asked to post a bond and 'keep the peace' in future."[4]

Joseph Merrill's land became the site of a Baptist church and cemetery. The first Baptist congregation in Bayham Township built in 1836 a large frame church that could seat five hundred people.[5] The sanctuary had a gallery around three sides in what was claimed to be "one of the finest Baptist churches west of York."[6] It may have been located near the creek to facilitate baptisms. Behind the church was a shed with twenty stalls for horses and oxen. The surrounding cemetery became the final resting place for many United Empire Loyalists.

Unfortunately, the early success of Estherville was not to last. Only a few schooners were built at the yard on the creek, and shipbuilding was soon transferred to Port Burwell, as it was actually on the lake. Estherville lasted for about fifteen to twenty years but faded into obscurity as Port Burwell grew.

In 1842, a council divided the Baptist congregation, and eighty people separated to form Malahide Jubilee Church, a name suggested by Merrill. He would die a few months later (see Lakeview). In 1855, another group of Baptists withdrew and built a new church at Calton. The Estherville structure was finally dismantled, and in 1856 the materials were donated to a Methodist congregation to complete its place of worship in Port Burwell. The other buildings in the community also disappeared in time, and the old hotel burned down.

In 1931, Wilfred and John Teall built a dance hall near the site of the old church. It was originally called Teall's Rendez-Vous, but a later owner renamed it Glen Erie. The hall had a stage and room to accommodate two hundred dancers and was not torn down until 1978. Concession 1, east of the intersection, has been renamed Glen Erie Line, but otherwise all that remains of the former shipbuilding

As with so many pioneer communities, all that remains of Estherville is a cemetery.

centre is a cemetery on the west side of the road. The church would have been found between the road and the cemetery. Tony Csinos has commemorated the site of the dance hall by placing a "Glen Erie" sign on its former location — right on his front lawn.

Firby

Firby might appropriately be referred to as a neighbourhood, not a village. It was an area settled primarily by the Firby family along the Bayham-Malahide Townline (now Springer Hill Road). In the nineteenth century, many families named Firby were located along the roads now known as Eden Line and Best Line to the north; the area had a chapel, sawmill, and cheese factory.

A Wesleyan Methodist church called "Benson's Chapple"[7] was built about 1837 on the northeast corner of the Townline and Best Line; some people called it Moss's Church because its location on the corner of the Moss family's farm. The cemetery was a mile south on the southeast corner of the Townline and Eden Line; the land for the cemetery was bought from Thomas Firby for five shillings in 1855.[8] The earliest grave marker, however, says 1850, so it is likely that the

Grave markers in Firby Cemetery. The site was originally purchased in 1855 for five shillings.

grounds were used before the deed was finalized. One burial at "Firby Cemetery" is that of Charlotte Mossman, who lived to be 109.

During the 1860s, Thomas Firby's son Robert operated a sawmill near the cemetery on the southeast corner of the southern intersection. Tremaine's *Map of the County of Elgin* of 1864 shows him as one of the largest landowners in the area. He hired many workers for his mill, all of whom probably lived in the vicinity.

The Bayham and Malahide Cheese Factory, also known as the Firby Cheese Factory, was built on Eden Line to the east on the south side of the road. It existed by 1896, operated by cheesemakers such as Isaac Pearson and Dan Leach. J. Wesley Pound bought it later but sold the enterprise to Dan Floto in 1899. A curing room in a separate building, 25 feet by 50 feet, had living quarters above it for the cheesemaker. Benson's Chapple was eventually moved south to become one of this factory's buildings. The plant was sold in 1904 to Canadian Milk Products, which later sold out to Borden's. This facility finally closed in the 1950s, the second-last cheese factory in Elgin.[9] Only Mapleton's cheese plant would continue to operate.

It is likely Firby was too close to the railway village of Corinth to ever amount to anything bigger. Today the abandoned cemetery is the only reminder of the early settlement.

Griffin's Corners

Businesses associated with this village, known first as Nelles' Corners and more recently as Froggett's Corners, stretched along Concession 4 (now Calton Line) from Bogus Road in the west to Toll Gate Road in the east. The main intersection, or "corners," was formed by Plank Road[10] and Calton Line, but the name was first attached to the intersection farther west.

The corner of Calton Line and Bogus Road was the original location of Nelles' Corners, named after John Nelles, who owned the land on the north side of the road in the mid-nineteenth century. Plank Road was not yet in place. Nelles owned a home and an inn here. About 1840 he donated land for SS No. 8 Bayham. This school was also used as a place of worship for the New Connexion Methodists.[11]

After the Plank Road was built, the focus of development moved to the newly created intersection with Calton Line. Jacob Griffin operated the Elgin Hotel, an inn on the northeast corner, about 1864. He also opened a general store in Straffordville and eventually moved it to this intersection as well. Later J. Godby, H. Bradfield, Lucy Mason, and J.W. Froggett operated the general store, though not always in the same building. A post office opened in 1880 under Jacob Griffin, after which the intersection became known as Griffin's Corners. He was postmaster until December 22, 1906. Others to follow included Cecil Marlatt, G.H. Godby, and J.C. Beckett.

After the Canadian Pacific Railway (CPR) line was built east of the main intersection, a small station was built — no. 1807, or Griffin's Station, and later Kinglake Station. The mail was dropped off there daily and could be picked up there also.

Other local industries included a cheese and butter factory built on the land of Saunder Griffin, west of the main corners on the south side of the road. It was in operation in 1896 and possibly earlier. Simon Spiece's sawmill was down Calton Line to the east at Toll Gate Road and burned down about 1900, when a boiler exploded in it. Another mill was owned by Lawrence Riley Stansell on the north side of the road across from the Spiece mill. Stansell was originally a shipbuilder who had worked in the shipyards at Port Burwell. The intersection of Calton Line and Toll Gate Road may have been the location of the Spiece Mills post office, operated by T. Spiece from 1900 to 1902.

Griffin's Corners was at its peak in the late nineteenth century, when along Calton Line were scattered Griffin's School, the cheese factory, store, post office, hotel, railway station, and mills. However, it is likely that there was no real need for a sizeable village between Straffordville and Vienna, even one on the railway. In the twentieth century the village disappeared; most buildings, such as the old hotel and mills, became outmoded. The post office closed December 31, 1914. The school burned down in 1896, to be replaced by a smaller, red-brick one as attendance dropped. The new school closed in 1956; it is still standing along Calton Line to the west on the north side and is used as a residence.

The Froggett family ran the store on the southwest corner of the intersection for about fifty years from about 1942 on, giving the intersection its most recent name of Froggett's Corners. This store had a service station and pool hall associated with it but was torn down about fifteen years ago. A trailer sits on the site today.

Still standing near Griffin's Corners, SS No. 8 Bayham is now a home.

Looking south along the abandoned railbed east of Griffin's Corners.

Maple Grove

Nineteenth-century Maple Grove was centred at Old Slanting Road (or Ridge Road, now Maple Grove Line) where it meets Stewart Road. The hamlet consisted of a church, a school, and one or possibly two mills to the north of them.

David Hatch walked to Colonel Talbot's residence at Port Talbot for the deed to the land that became known as Maple Grove. On the north side of Maple Grove Line, Hatch's School was built before 1850; it was replaced in 1860 by a frame structure and in 1875 by a red-brick one — SS No. 17 Bayham, Maple Grove School.

The first Methodist services in the area were held in this school in the 1850s. Then, when a frame New Connexion church in Straffordville fell into disuse, settlers at Maple Grove purchased it and moved it to a lot just west of the school. David Hatch and

William Bowes initiated this move in 1871, and the church was rededicated for use in 1874. It became part of a five-part charge that included North Hall, Eden, Straffordville, and Guysboro in Norfolk County. The original edifice was replaced by a yellow-brick building in 1900, and the congregation became part of the United Church of Canada in 1925.

There was a gristmill in the neighbourhood on the north side of Otter Creek on the Goodrich property. After Laura Goodrich married the mill foreman, John Fraser, the area became known as Fraser Valley. About 1857, David Dean bought the south end of the Hatch property and established grist and sawmills; it is not clear now if these are the same mills from the former Goodrich holdings.

Maple Grove Church closed in 1948 and remained standing for a while with its windows broken or boarded up; children used to comb its grounds for bits of broken, coloured glass.[12] About 1950, George Moore bought the structure and used its materials to build a house in the south part of Eden. The school closed at Easter, 1951, and was sold and moved to Brock Street in Tillsonburg to become an Orange Lodge; it has since burned. The nearby Stewart farm was the site of a Maple Grove School Reunion in July 2000.

McCurdy's Corners

The name McCurdy's Corners refers to the intersection of Tunnel Line and Stafford Road. Initially known primarily as the Otter Valley Settlement, the hamlet consisted of a sawmill, hotel, school, and church.

The community developed around the sawmill belonging to Richard McCurdy. He owned a large portion of land on the southwest corner of this intersection in the mid-nineteenth century. At first, his mill was operated with a water-powered vertical saw, but, as business grew, he went over to steam power. George Brasher built a hotel or boarding-house nearby[13] in the 1890s, and a school, SS No. 5 Bayham, was constructed down the road, to the west on the south side. It was later moved farther west, to a new location on the north side of the road.

More has been recorded about the church than about anything else in the community. It too was located to the west but not as far as the school, built on land donated by Jesse Corliss. About 1834, the small frame building was opened to all denominations, and it remained so until 1874. At that time a Baptist named Elder Fitch, who was in charge of the church at Port Burwell, is said to have acquired this place of worship for his own denomination. Seemingly Fitch went to visit Corliss who was on his deathbed and convinced him to sign a document transferring the deed to him. It is suggested that Corliss did not know what he was signing. Ultimately, the building became McCurdy Church, and Mr. McCurdy is reputed to have put a lot of "time and effort" into it until 1901, despite an apparent feud with a Pastor Walker.

Pastor Walker had been in charge of the church for only a short time when two Moravian[14] women asked for permission to hold a special service there. Walker objected to anyone but his own denomination using the building and was backed by Elder King of Port Burwell, who also refused to open the facility when the Moravians arrived. This decision split the congregation, and many members were upset by Walker's actions. Some invited a new minister, Reverend Sanderson of Vienna, to come and hold services once a week in McCurdy School. After some persuasion, he accepted, and in the first part of 1905 the church split into two factions, with the deacons of both sides accusing the other of selfishness. Walker was eventually dismissed but continued to preach outside after the doors were locked against him, delivering harsh sermons against the opposing deacons. His actions led to a brawl among various members on September 24, 1905, and blood was spilled on the altar. A church trial was held before Reverend Norton of the local Baptist Mission Board, and an assault case was brought before the local magistrate before all was settled.[15]

The Baptist church was demolished in 1938, and all that remains is the Otter Valley Cemetery, set back in the trees on the south side of the road. The school closed in June 1956, when a new central school opened in Vienna.

Preserved grave markers at Otter Valley Cemetery.

North Hall

This hamlet, at the intersection of Forge Road (now Talbot Line) and Eden Line, began as a religious centre. Some people will argue that it has not truly vanished, but most of its businesses are closed and its buildings deserted. The corner has a rather "ghostly" look.

New Connexion Methodist circuit riders held services at Dobbie's Schoolhouse along Forge Line to the east, near the site of Dobbie's Cemetery. Eventually this school closed, and the building became a Bible school; it was never officially a church. Later, services took place at a red-brick Templar Hall.[16] The structure had a large wood stove in the centre and three tiers of wooden benches facing each other on each long wall. The pulpit was at the far end from the door. Men sat on one side, and women on the other. Once the stove started emitting heat it became too hot inside, and the minister would remove his coat and "preach in his shirt sleeves of multi-hued checked flannel."[17] This building was in use from 1864 to 1876, but, since it was cramped and poorly ventilated, the congregation ceased to worship there, and the structure later became an Orange Hall.

A new place of worship was under construction west of the intersection in 1876, with bricks and wood being brought to the site by local farmers who lived along Forge Road. Reverend David Savage, pastor of Tillsonburg Methodist Church, organized this project. The new church officially opened in the autumn of 1876 but was not completed until two years later. A new building was constructed very close to the same site in 1907; the congregation celebrated its golden anniversary in 1928.

North Hall is said to have been an important early service centre until it was no longer able to compete with the larger towns of Tillsonburg and Aylmer. It is now nearly impossible to determine how many businesses it had in the early days. There was a cooper shop on the south side of the road and a blacksmith shop nearby, both east of the church. The hamlet's name is said to have come from a community hall that stood on the south side of the highway — perhaps the Templar Hall? The word "North" may refer to the fact that the edifice was located in the northern part of Bayham Township.

An automobile service station with a dance hall upstairs existed there in the first half of the twentieth century. This building burned down when owned by Mr. and Mrs. George Knabb, but it was rebuilt after the fire in 1934. Earl Greer then bought the property; at the time there were a few tourist cabins nearby. He built more cabins and a garage, which was operated over the years by different mechanics, including Don Shearer and Tom Edgar. Greer also expanded the original business to include a store, lunch bar, restaurant, and larger living quarters for himself and his wife, Leta. He went on to become the most prominent business person of the area.

When the North Hall Church closed in 1935, due to dwindling attendance, Charles Laister of Tillsonburg bought the building for $125 cash and Earl Greer bought the land it was on for $42.[18] Greer had a lawn-and-garden-equipment business as well, which he operated with Leta and son-in-law Murray Holden. By the late 1930s, he also had an outdoor boxing ring that attracted participants and spectators from miles around. Even some travelling professionals from a considerable distance away would come to participate in this popular sport.

In 1952, Earl and Leta sold the service station to Harold Bennett and moved to a new house west of the church. Later Albert Quelch

North Hall Restaurant is now closed, as are many other local businesses.

owned the station, and in the 1970s Jiggs and Joy Morse took over. By May 1972 North Hall had two service stations with restaurants — one on the north side of the road owned by the Morses and one on the south side, with a motel as well, owned and operated by Tom Nedozytko.

Today, the Morse business, North Hall Restaurant, is closed, along with the garage beside it and Greer's Lawn and Garden Equipment business. The motel on the south side of the road is now a flea market. The church has been torn down. There may be as many people living at North Hall as there ever were, but the business community has nearly disappeared and the old buildings have an abandoned look.

Saxtontown

Just west of a bend on Otter Creek between Port Burwell and Vienna was a place *intended* as a village. William Saxton and his wife, Margaret Edison, attempted to found a village there in the 1820s. A number of lots were given to interested individuals on the condition that they improve them, and a road was surveyed to the site along a line between farms but never opened.[19] A few homes were built, but the village was doomed to failure. Larger centres, such as Port Burwell and Vienna, were not far away, and there was little need for another one in between.

Spiece Mills (see Griffin's Corners)

Willsonburg

This mill village was northeast of the modern village of Richmond on Otter Creek. The pioneers recognized the spot as an excellent source of waterpower for a mill, and a Mr. Birdsall built the first gristmill in the area as early as 1831.

Then along came Ambrose Willson. Originally from Pelham, near Niagara, he established a new gristmill and a sawmill as well. Later he would build a woollen mill on the north side of the creek, opposite the gristmill. And it was around these structures that a little village developed as soon as Willson could lay out lots. Soon he opened a general store as well, where Andrew Moore was the

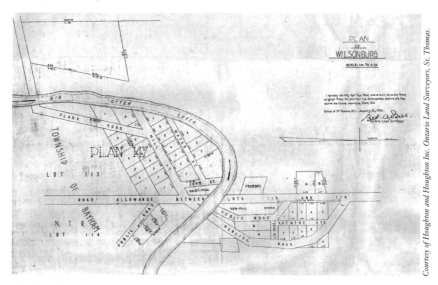

A plan of the village of Willsonburg (spelled here with one "l") as it appeared c. 1854, showing locations of various businesses. This plan was redrawn by surveyor Fred Bell in 1931.

manager. The store's main purpose was to cater to the mill hands. Also founded by Willson, and next to the store, was the Willson House hotel, which housed workers and visitors alike. There was also a butcher shop and blacksmith nearby. Willson became wealthy and prominent by pioneer standards and in 1853 he was elected reeve of Bayham Township.

The best-known business at the spot was Willson's gristmill. It eventually passed to Richard Simmons, who in turn sold it to George Procunier in 1873 for $7,000.[20] Procunier and his sons Robert and James set up the firm of G.N. Procunier and Sons. They were quite successful for many years, operating their mill day and night, hauling their flour to Corinth by the wagonload, and shipping it by railway to destinations as far away as Montreal and Halifax. Unfortunately, the building burned down in 1882. The Procuniers rebuilt it but in time sold it to Robert Knott. He operated the enterprise for thirty years as Knott's Mill. It was still running as recently as 1930, under the ownership of Richard McCurdy.

This mill outlived all other businesses at Willsonburg. The sawmill ceased operating when the local timber supply was depleted, possibly sometime after 1910. The woollen mill closed as well. With fewer mill workers in the neighbourhood, the other businesses, such as the store and hotel, were less needed and ultimately closed. The village that might have outgrown nearby Richmond soon disappeared completely, having had a life span of only about twenty-five years. A flood in 1937 carried away much of the remains of the sawmill.

However, Willson's gristmill was still standing in 1950. By then it was owned by local residents Mr. and Mrs. Hanlon Pritchard, Mrs. Pritchard having inherited it from her father, Richard McCurdy. It has since been torn down.

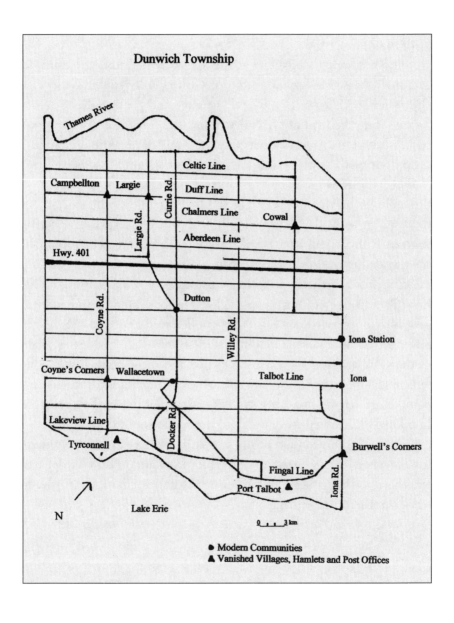

Dunwich Township

Thames River

Celtic Line

Campbellton   Largie   Currie Rd.   Duff Line

Largie Rd.   Chalmers Line   Cowal

Aberdeen Line

Hwy. 401

Coyne Rd.   Dutton

Willey Rd.   Iona Station

Coyne's Corners   Wallacetown   Talbot Line   Iona

Lakeview Line   Docker Rd.

Tyrconnell   Burwell's Corners

Fingal Line

Iona Rd.

Port Talbot

N   Lake Erie   0 ▪ ▪ ▪ 3 km

● Modern Communities
▲ Vanished Villages, Hamlets and Post Offices

Chapter Three

Township of Dunwich

Dunwich, Elgin's earliest settled township and the home of Colonel Talbot, was formed in 1792. Lieutenant-Governor Simcoe and his staff named it, probably after the town of Dunwich in Suffolk County, England, and its Canadian counterpart was at first in a county called Suffolk. The English Dunwich is not far from a village called Southwold, and in Canada, Southwold and Dunwich townships lie side by side in Elgin. The English town of Dunwich was a thriving port about the year 1300 but gradually eroded into the sea. Three churches and four hundred houses were swept away by a storm in 1326, and over the centuries the sea has almost completely submerged the area. Dunwich means probably "place by deep water,"[1] so it's a good name for a township on the shore of one of the Great Lakes.

Many of the earliest settlers in southern Dunwich Township were United Empire Loyalists or later migrants from the United States. Most of the people who settled the northern part of the township were from Scotland. In January 1998, Dunwich and the village of Dutton joined to form the municipality of Dutton-Dunwich.

Burwell's Corners

The corner of Fingal Line and Iona Road was once the home of Colonel Talbot's right-hand man, Colonel Mahlon Burwell. It was there that Burwell presided as the Talbot Settlement's first registrar.

But the corners contained more — a church, a post office, and later a cheese factory as well.

Mahlon Burwell was born February 18, 1783, on Long Island, New York, the youngest of the nine children born to Adam and Sarah Burwell, whose property was confiscated when the couple supported the British during the American Revolution.[2] Fleeing to Canada as United Empire Loyalists, they at first settled in Bertie Township, Welland County, in 1784 but stayed there for only a few years before moving to Long Point in Norfolk County. In 1810, Mahlon married Sarah Haun of Niagara-on-the-Lake; they eventually had seven sons and two daughters.

In 1811, on Talbot's rec-ommendation, the young Bur-well became registrar of deeds for the County of Middlesex, which included the territory that later would become El-gin. He built a log house for his family (the structure also designed to hold the first reg-istry office) on the flats of Tal-bot Creek, a little upstream from where Colonel Talbot constructed his first home (see Port Talbot). His parents also lived with the family.

Then came the War of 1812. Burwell was lieutenant-colonel of the First Middlesex Militia. In 1814, the enemy destroyed Talbot's mills and the Burwell home and registry office. Burwell was captured and taken to Chilicothe, Ohio, where he was in prison for several months. Sarah, her home gone, made a shelter the best she could for her father- and mother-in-law, and then went with her two little sons to Iona, just north of their homestead, to seek refuge. She later sent for Mahlon's parents to join her.[3]

When Burwell returned in 1815, he built a temporary log home

Courtesy of Elgin County Museum.

Colonel Mahlon Burwell.

on the east side of the townline at what was later Burwell's Corners. A frame house very shortly replaced the log one. The story goes that Burwell received the money to construct his house from a Mr. Harris of Iona, who told him not to stint on building supplies as Burwell could pay him back when he received money.[4] Burwell put up a fine dwelling, which also housed the registry office. It was there that the business transactions of the Talbot Settlement were carried out for the next ten years.

Illustrated Historical Atlas of the County of Elgin.

RESIDENCE OF EDWARD BURWELL.
1 ST CONCESSION SOUHT OF TALBOT ST. LOT 4 TOWNSHIP OF SOUHTWOLD
COUNTY OF ELGIN, ONT.

The estate of Edward Burwell, originally that of Mahlon and Sarah Burwell, as pictured in 1877.

In 1825, Burwell gave this house to his son Edward and built a large brick residence on the Dunwich side of the townline, on the northwest corner of the intersection. His new home had a high, projecting central part, flanked by lower wings on either side. The south wing was the third location of the registry office of Middlesex County and served as such until it was moved to London in 1843.

As a provincial land surveyor from 1809 to 1846, Mahlon Burwell laid out much of southwestern Ontario in roads and lots. Between 1815 and 1824, he was responsible for marking out over twenty townships in Haldimand, Norfolk, Elgin, Kent, and Essex. In Elgin, he surveyed the townships of Bayham, Malahide, Southwold, and northern Yarmouth, as well as the Talbot Road, which stretches

St. Stephen's Anglican Church at Burwell's Corners.

through Elgin County from east to west. All these surveys cleared the way for later settlement. As Burwell was paid for his work partly in cash and partly in land, he built up large holdings in various parts of Upper Canada, especially in the southwest.

Thus, it is not surprising to learn that Burwell owned much of the land around his house, including the four two-hundred-acre farms that were located around the four corners of the main intersection. In 1836, he donated the land on the southwest corner on which St. Stephen's Anglican Church sits. When he died on January 25, 1846, he was buried in the adjoining churchyard. At the time of his death, Talbot commented, "He was my best helper, my best friend."[5] Sarah Burwell died in 1870 and was buried beside her husband.

Burwell was postmaster at Burwell's Corners from 1820 until his death, although the post office was actually called Port Talbot. After he died, his wife took over for a time. The facility was then relocated to John Clark's farm just south of the corners. A cheese factory also existed on the west side of the intersection from 1870, operated by Nathan, John Clark's son, who later sold it to William Bobier of Wallacetown.

Just to the north of Burwell's Corners is a prehistoric vanished village. The Southwold Earthworks are all that remain of an

Remains of the double palisade at Southwold Prehistoric Earthworks. The preservation of this Attawandaron site was in part due to the foresight of Mahlon Burwell.

Attawandaron (or Neutral) double-walled village, dating from about AD 1500. The site is the only structure of its kind in Canada, although there is something similar near Rochester, New York. Only the earthen foundation of the palisade still exists. Discovered in 1827, the site had been well hidden in a dense wood and had trees growing on its embankments. Burwell's foresight saved it from the plough; when he sold the lot, he inserted a clause that the prehistoric fort was not to be demolished but preserved for future generations.[6]

The site was taken over by the National Parks System in 1930, the fulfilment of a long-time ambition of the Elgin Historical and Scientific Society and its first president, Dr. James H. Coyne (see Coyne's Corners). A large crowd gathered on September 16 of that year, and local schoolchildren received half a day's holiday to attend and see a monument being unveiled. D.J. Wittemburg of the Canadian National Museum, Ottawa, stressed the importance of preventing irresponsible collectors from digging for relics.[7] Wittemburg excavated the site in 1935 with his assistant, Dr. Wilfrid Jury, and a second dig took place in 1976. There was no evidence of enemy attack or European visitors,

The lichen-covered graves of Mahlon and Sarah Burwell at St. Stephen's Cemetery. The commemorative plaque was added by the Elgin Historical Society in 2002.

but occupation lasted probably for only one generation. The works may have had as many as eight hundred inhabitants, making it larger than most of the historic vanished villages of Elgin combined.

Another monument, a cairn, was placed at the Burwell's Corners intersection in 1924 by the Elgin Historical and Scientific Society to commemorate Burwell's registry office; it still sits on the west side of the road nearby. Burwell's houses are long gone, as are all the other early buildings around the intersection, except for St. Stephen's Church and its cemetery, where Mahlon and Sarah are buried. The Elgin County Historical Society placed a plaque by their graves in 2002.

Campbellton

This hamlet — sometimes spelled "Campbelltown," but officially "Campbellton" — was at the corner of Concession 3 Dunwich (now Duff Line) and Coyne Road. It was never large but had most of the necessary services required by early settlers.

Robert Campbell, the first settler, took up land on the northeast corner in 1855. He donated sufficient property to accommodate the church, a school, and a store, so the new community took his name. It is said, however, that Campbell named the village after Campbeltown, Kintyre, Scotland, which may have been his original home.[8] The Scottish town was named after Archibald Campbell, Earl of Argyle, who was granted land there in the seventeenth century.[9]

About 1858, Neil McBride built a general store on the corner of Campbell's farm at Coyne Road. A Mr. McKeracher bought the store in 1881, then sold it twelve years later to John Searle. Other owners were Samuel Snowden, John Gill, and A.C. Turner. The post office opened August 1, 1875, under Neil McBride. Later postmasters were Mary McKeracher, John Searle, Samuel Snowden, John Gill, A.C. Turner, George Percival, and Mary McPherson. The McKillops of West Lorne took mail to Campbellton once a week, and eventually delivery took place three times a week.

Near the store was a blacksmith shop built in 1875 by John Buchanan. He charged 13¢ for a set of horseshoes and $1 for a wagon tongue.[10] The smithy burned in 1881 but was rebuilt and continued to serve the area until 1885. In the 1890s, a Grange[11] operated in the community, as did a Temperance Lodge, in the north corner of the schoolyard. In 1886, Jane McPherson organized a singing school attended by many residents.

The first log school was constructed about 1859, north on Celtic Line and west of the intersection. As this location was not central enough for most settlers' children, land was purchased from Robert Campbell on the east side of the road, north of the intersection. A frame structure erected there served the community until the 1880s, when it was replaced by a new one. The front verandah was the setting for the annual Campbellton Garden parties, one of which was held as recently as 1951.[12]

In 1869, St. John's Presbyterian Church went up to the south of Campbellton School, the land having been purchased from Robert Campbell for $10.[13] At one time twenty-five to thirty families attended this church, but in 1889 it was closed and the remaining members of the congregation went either to Duff's Presbyterian Church at

Courtesy of Archives of Ontario F2178-1-0-17.

Campbellton General Store and Post Office, c. 1900.

Largie or to the church at Dutton. The original structure is now part of the barn at Norman McWilliam's farm.

Campbellton store closed about 1920 and was sold to Harry Miles. The building burned in August 1921. Harry was fortunate to escape through a window, but the building, stock, and contents were all destroyed.[14] The post office, which had been in the home of Isabel Percival since 1920, closed April 30, 1930, and the postal service became RR No. 5, Dutton. The school was closed in 1966 and was purchased and renovated as a residence — the only extant reminder of the nineteenth-century hamlet of Campbellton.

Cowal

Cowal started out at two different locations. The Cowal post office was founded near the community cemeteries at Iona Road and Aberdeen Line. Some years later it was relocated to Cowal Road and Concession 4 (now Chalmers Line), originally known as New Montreal.

Neil McBride and his wife came from Cowal, Scotland, in 1833 and settled on a farm on the east side of the Dutton/Southwold Townline near Aberdeen Line. McBride opened the first Cowal post office in his house on December 1, 1863, naming it after his home. On Saturday mornings he would strike out on horseback and collect the mail from Fingal, and when he returned he would blow a large horn to let settlers know the mail was in.[15] Grant Silcox took over as postmaster on November 1, 1871, and kept the office in a general store built in 1869 on the northwest corner of the townline and Aberdeen Line. In 1875, James McDougall acquired the store and post office and proceeded to move the business to New Montreal. Silcox's store was moved across the road and became a part of John McBride's farmhouse.

The first settlers at the New Montreal intersection were Hugh and Margaret McCallum.[16] Hugh was a shoemaker, but he also opened the first general store in the area. The reason for the name New Montreal is not known, but possibly McCallum or another early settler came from Montreal, Quebec. When James McDougall arrived, he took over the store building already in existence. After the Cowal post office was established there, the village gradually took on this name; Page's 1877 *Illustrated Historical Atlas*, for example, gives it as New Montreal but calls the post office Cowal.[17] Later postmasters included John Bottin, John Thompson, Daniel Thompson, J.A. McGugan, Alex McLachlan, and R. (possibly he was Reuben) Adams.

As in many other communities, one of the earliest buildings to be erected was a church. Initially people had conducted services in one another's homes or, during the warmer months, beneath a canopy of trees, using logs for seats. On July 6, 1852, Hugh Fletcher held a public meeting at his home to discuss building a Presbyterian church. The founding congregation included people living across the Thames in Ekfrid Township, Middlesex County. Although the dedication service was held in 1856, there was no regular minister until Reverend John Stuart came in 1865. He accepted a salary of $400 a year.[18] The original Chalmers Presbyterian was somewhat north of where the present church stands. Up until 1870, all services were conducted in Gaelic, reflecting the Scottish ancestry of many early settlers.

Church members living in Middlesex County had to row across the Thames, at the north end of Cowal Sideroad, in a scow, or flat-bottomed boat — they took the scow, ferried the river, and left the boat tied on the other side. However, if people wanted to cross and the scow was on the opposite side, they had to shout until someone there heard them and rowed it over to them.[19] The boat

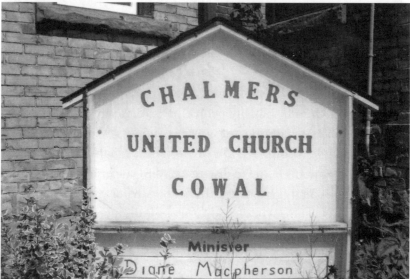

Chalmers United Church, Cowal, built 1901, is still used for Sunday services.

was large enough to transport livestock, teams, and wagons and was guided by a heavy rope secured between trees on either bank. After Chalmers Church was built, the scow was used quite heavily on Sunday mornings as members from as far away as Melbourne relied on it. Eventually a wooden bridge was constructed, but a combination of ice build-up and spring floods usually ripped off its floor planks, which had to be replaced annually. The bridge was finally abandoned about 1930.

It was not until 1873 that the Ekfrid part of the congregation separated and became connected with a more conveniently located church in Middlesex County. A new connection was made with Duff's Presbyterian Church at Largie, which lasted for twenty-five years. However, about 1900, the Duff's and Chalmers congregations separated. It was felt at that time that Chalmers was a bit too small, so a new church was built on a lot donated by Daniel Thompson on the northeast corner of the intersection. In 1901, it cost $4,000 to build.[20] The architect was Neil R. Darrach, well-known for his work in St. Thomas.[21] Most members joined the United Church of Canada in 1925, although some Presbyterians left to join other Presbyterian churches and a separate Chalmers Presbyterian congregation began using the same building on Sunday afternoons. About 1940, the few remaining Presbyterians joined Knox Church in Dutton, and Chalmers became strictly United.

The cemeteries at Cowal were not beside the church but back at the original village location, two miles to the east, where Neil McBride had started the post office. Cowal Cemetery opened in 1854 on the northwest corner of the townline and Aberdeen Line near the site where Silcox's store would later be built, on land donated by John McCallum. McCallum had discovered that his property had deep sand deposits more suitable for graves than for farming. The first burial occurred that year when Nancy McTavish, wife of John McTavish, died. But there is also a stone for Peter McNabb who died aged one year and four months in February 1852; perhaps he was buried elsewhere first and the remains were later moved to this site.

In 1898, another cemetery opened on the opposite side of the road, on the southwest corner, and became known as McBride's

Cemetery, as it was on the farm of John McBride. The first interment was McTavish's second wife, Christine. In 1938, these two burial grounds were united under the name Cowal-McBride Cemetery, and since then the cemetery has been enlarged.

The school closest to Cowal was SS No. 9 Dunwich, on the Duff Line to the west of Cowal Sideroad. The original school was built about 1855, a crude structure of logs plastered on the outside, with only one window and rough planks along the walls for seats. About 1869, a substantially better frame building was erected a little to the east on a hill. Regrettably, this burned in 1870, and a replacement went up, which served until 1892. That year, at a meeting of the local school authorities, a decision was made to shift the structure about 500 feet west. Land was purchased from Archibald C. Campbell for $75, and the school was moved and exterior bricked. One morning, however, the pupils arrived to discover the entire front portion of the brick had fallen off. The school was rebricked by a different contractor.[22]

Cowal developed a substantial business community in the nineteenth century and was at its peak from about 1880 to 1900. A visitor to Cowal, on taking a walk down Main Street (now Cowal Road), would see the first store on the southwest corner. It was opened about 1870 by James McDougall.

John Thompson bought the general store in 1886 and sold groceries, shoes, hardware, and dry goods. This was also the site of the post office throughout much of its history. South of this store was the village sawmill. In 1871, this mill was operated by Richard (Dick) Redmond and William Lipsey, and lumber was shipped out by railway from Lawrence Station. After Lipsey's death, Redmond sold out to Thomas Griffin in 1882. This was a thriving business, with farmers from miles around hauling in lumber year round.

By 1884, the mill business was doing so well that extra workers had to be hired to saw 4,000–8,000 feet of lumber a day.[23] Houses to accommodate these employees were built along Concession 4, west of the store on the southwest corner, as well as to the east, across the road from the church. The field on the northwest corner of the intersection was rented by the sawmill for the storage of logs brought in by farmers in winter. Business in 1884 was so good that a grain crusher was installed at the mill as well.

When the store on the southwest corner burned in 1906, it was not rebuilt, and Thomas Griffin put up a replacement to the south the following year; the Griffin house was just to its north. After Thomas died, his wife, Jane, continued to run this store, and after her death their son Tom kept it going for a while. In the early days it was the general meeting place, where residents met to discuss the crops, the weather, and politics or just catch up on local news.

Crossing over to the east side of the road would take a visitor on to a stave mill that employed up to ten men. It was operated by Joseph Atkinson, who had been in the barrel stave and hoop business at Cashmere,[24] but when in 1898 one of the area's frequent floods washed away a large stack of finished staves, along with his whole stock of logs, he decided to leave. Instead he decided to leave Cashmere and to rent Thomas Griffin's sawmill. To go into the stave business, Atkinson had lumber cut at the sawmill, then soaked overnight to remove the bark, then taken across the road to the stave mill to be shaped. A Mr. Coates of Ridgetown purchased this stave mill in 1902. He invested in extensive alterations and built new homes for the mill workers. The staves were taken to Lawrence Station and shipped by railway to companies making barrels.

North of the stave mill was a boarding house, where mill workers lived. Next was a shoemaker's shop, operated in 1885 by R.M. Chapman, and over the ensuing years by several other owners. North of this was a carriage factory, which had various operators over time. Next door was the first blacksmith shop in Cowal, built in the 1880s by James McKenzie. Later owners were Robert M. Martin, Norton Peckham, Robert March, and Peter McKenzie. To the north was another blacksmith shop, erected by Herbert Myers in the 1890s. Myers was an excellent blacksmith who once set a record for the number of horses he could shoe in one day.[25] Still further north, on the southeast corner of the intersection, across from the church, there was another store, operated over the years by Malcolm Gilmore, D.A. McNabb, John Battin, and Jim McBride. The community of Cowal also had a Foresters Lodge and a Templars Lodge, each with over fifty members in the 1880s.

Page's *Illustrated Historical Atlas of Elgin* of 1877 describes Cowal as "yet a small village and its streets are paved with sawdust ... its conveniences, however, of stores, post office, shops &c., can only be fully appreciated by those who have heretofore been obliged to go for these, many, muddy, 'lang Scotch miles.'"[26] No doubt the sawdust came from the sawmill. Roads in those days were so bad, many having been built through swampy ground, that they were often corduroyed with logs and covered with sawdust.

Cowal Hall was constructed originally on the wrong corner and had to be moved. Guy Lombardo performed here.

In 1891, Cowal was large and prosperous enough to warrant a public hall (Cowal Hall), on the same corner where the church stands today. Shortly after the hall was opened, it was discovered that the Chalmers Presbyterian congregation had plans for a new church on that very site. Thus, in the spring of 1902 Daniel Patterson donated land on the southwest corner where the hall is now, and the building was lifted and moved. In 1930, a stage and basement were added.

The public hall was a centre for many parties and dances over the years. It was noted that Guy Lombardo played there when he and his band were first starting out.[27] Men paid 25¢ admission at these events, but there was no charge for women. During the war years, dances were held at the hall every month and the proceeds given to help the war effort. The Women's Institute also met once a month and sponsored card parties there. It is quite likely that the lodges mentioned above held their meetings there as well.

Without warning, this prosperous little community was struck by disaster. As was noted above, the industrial base of Cowal consisted of the mills that employed most of the population, about fifty people. In 1903, both of the mills burned in a fire. Griffin, who still owned the sawmill, decided not to rebuild. Mr. Coates, operator of the stave mill, decided to move the business and equipment to Dutton, which was on the rail line. Afterwards the workers left as well, many following Coates to Dutton. Some moved their houses with them, others left them behind to gradually decay and collapse. The post office closed January 1, 1913, with rural mail delivery now having been put in place. By the 1930s, only the Griffin family store, the hall, the church, and three houses remained. In the long run, even without the fires, Cowal would have declined once its timber resources were depleted.

Cowal's sense of community did not disappear overnight. Young men in the area organized a Cowal baseball team before the First World War and spent evenings practising at John Campbell's pasture field beside SS No. 9. The boys played against teams from the communities of Muncey and Lawrence Station. After the war, softball became even more popular with both boys and girls. The Elgin Junior Institute had a softball league, and there were four teams in Dunwich Township — Iona Station, Largie, Coyne's Corners, and Cowal. Games were played on the school grounds until a lot was purchased in Cowal itself in 1926 and a proper baseball diamond created by local fellows. Two tennis courts were also marked on the playground and were used until the nets burned in a house fire.[28]

In 1925, some women taking a bread-making course at Reuben Adams's house on the northeast corner decided to form a Women's Institute branch. The organizational meeting was held at Cowal Hall on May 5 of that year.

Each year in May, the Farmers Club held its Annual Consignment Sale. This event became so important that it took the name "Cowal Civic Holiday."[29] At the sale, local farmers, through the Farmers

Club, sold their cattle, pigs, and horses. Stockyards were constructed just west of Cowal Hall on the farm of Daniel Patterson. The event was looked forward to especially by schoolchildren, who received a holiday to attend. The women of the Institute provided full-course dinners for visitors — 25¢ a plate, children free.[30]

An event at Cowal in 1946 gained international coverage. On January 29 Phil Campbell was on his way across his farm when he noticed in the distance a figure dressed all in white, walking with a slight limp across the fields. It seemed to be wearing a hood or parka and looked like a woman. The neighbours organized a search, since they feared this unknown person might be mentally unhinged. Students at SS No. 9 were sent home in case the individual turned out to be dangerous. Local men followed the tracks in the snow over ravines and fields and eventually along a woven-wire fence. Suddenly the tracks stopped. A short distance ahead some Aboriginal men were cutting wood and, when told of the purpose of the search party, stated they hadn't seen anything. The *Toronto Star* heard about the "Cowal ghost" and sent a reporter and photographer to cover the story, printing a big spread, with pictures of local children holding sharp axes and so on to defend themselves. The *Maple Leaf*, the armed forces newspaper, picked up the tale, and servicemen from the Cowal area still on duty overseas were astonished to discover their home village in the news.

Years passed before a young local man named George admitted he had been out illegally hunting deer that day, using a prohibited, high-powered rifle that was unregistered — a crime during a time when the War Measures Act was still in force. When his tracks stopped, it was because he had climbed onto the wire fence and stepped sideways along it to where his Native friends were cutting wood. He swore them to secrecy, hid his clothes and gun under some timber, and started splitting wood along with them. He was limping because he had hidden his gun in his boot, which affected his walking.[31]

By the 1960s, Cowal was experiencing renewed prosperity. Buried some 3,600 feet below the surface was oil worth about $3.25 a barrel. Imperial Oil pumped locally from one well at a rate of about two hundred barrels a day. But, as a local newspaper put it in 1968, "For Cowal, the unexpected prosperity may have come a bit too late."[32]

The article reported that the village's annual cattle auction was a thing of the past (it had ended in 1961) and that the cattle pens were falling down and had tall grass and weeds growing in them.

Little remains at Cowal to remind us of the bustling village of the past. The hall is still on the southwest corner, and the church on the northeast. SS No. 9 was sold in 1966 and torn down in 1975. The cemeteries, of course, are still there on Iona Road.

Coyne's Corners

Coyne's Corners was at the corner of Talbot Line and Coyne Road and took its name from Henry Coyne, an early pioneer and proprietor of a hotel.

Coyne was born in 1774 on the Isle of Man but moved to Ireland as a boy. There he met and married Anna Gardiner with whom he eventually had eight children. In 1810 they sailed to New York. Being known to side with the British when the War of 1812 broke out, the Coynes were ordered to move one hundred miles back from the frontier. They proceeded up the Hudson River to a village called Pleasant Valley near Newburgh and stayed there until the end of the war. Anti-British sentiment in the United States prompted them to set out for Upper Canada, their belongings packed in a wagon. They arrived first in the Niagara area, then proceeded to the Talbot Settlement, arriving there in 1817.

One of their sons was James H. Coyne, Elgin County historian[33] (see Burwell's Corners), and another was Thomas, who kept store at Tyrconnell.[34] Two of Anna's brothers were Thomas Gardiner, probably Elgin's first schoolteacher (see Tyrconnell), and Singleton Gardiner.[35]

Henry Coyne was a crusader for settlers' rights and resisted what he saw as unreasonable authority. For example, as a Methodist he resented the fact that only the Church of England had the right to perform marriages and baptisms. Coyne also was not an admirer of Colonel Thomas Talbot's autocratic style, especially his withholding from settlers land they thought was rightfully theirs. At first Coyne himself was granted only fifty acres instead of the usual two hundred, because he had come from the United States, not directly from

Britain. However, Talbot eventually sold him an additional fifty acres as Coyne had a large family to support.[36]

Henry, Anna, and the children first acquired land west of the Coyne's Corners intersection on the south side of the road. Later, in 1824, they moved to the east side of the intersection, still on the south side. Henry at first took up farming but eventually opened an inn. The need for accommodation was great, as many potential settlers would spend the night there in order to arrive at Port Talbot at an appropriate time to meet with Colonel Talbot. The inn also became a meeting place where settlers came to chat and find entertainment. As early as 1827, Colonel Burwell had called a meeting at Coyne's home to establish a mail stagecoach and passenger route from St. Thomas to Amherstburg,[37] although it is not certain whether the inn was already standing. By 1842, Henry had sold part of the southeast corner lot to his son Isaac, and by 1845 Isaac had established a new hotel there.

Competitors would be built at the intersection. John McGugan established a hotel on the northeast corner in 1853, while Donald G. Gunn constructed one west of the corners on the south side of the road. In the 1840s and 1850s, it was not uncommon to see sixty teams of oxen or horses at one hotel alone.[38]

There were also two blacksmiths; one shop was operated by a Mr. Ritchie on the south side of the road, and the other, on the north side, by a black man named Mr. Rossie. It is likely he was a refugee from the United States, but records do not indicate whether he was a fugitive slave or a free man. After Coyne's Corners failed, he is said to have moved to Dresden in Kent County.

The land across from Donald Gunn's hotel, belonging to Daniel McGugan, was long used as a training ground for the local volunteer militia. On one occasion the trainees from Aldborough and Dunwich were staying separately at two of these hotels. The Aldborough group had a fine silk flag that it had left rolled up outside the hotel. While the men were inside drinking, their rivals put a cut in the flag so that when it was unfurled it was in ribbons. Challenges were raised for a duel between the two companies and two powerfully built men, identified only as Thompson and McKellor, volunteered to fight. However, all the men joined in the fray that ensued. Luckily, no one was killed. The losers jumped on their horses and fled, but it is not recorded which township lost the fight.[39]

Coyne's Corners had an early school, which Henry Coyne is said to have helped establish, probably because he wanted his own children to attend. Much has been written about the many locations and various teachers of the early log schools; the site was always moving, schools often burned down, sometimes classes were held in settlers' homes. Many of these early schools had grown men and women attending during winter.

It was recorded that at Coyne's Corners one teacher's punishment for unruly children was to send them to the creek to "dip it dry."[40] Another teacher named Abraham Lehigh (his name is also spelled as Leahy, Leahigh, and Leigheigh) was described by a local writer as a "silly old Yankee."[41] Yet another description of him states, "his only qualification was his cheek. His education was of the most meager character, yet such was the difficulty of getting teachers that he was employed for four or five years."[42] Another early teacher was John Thompson, a military man who is said to have whipped children cruelly.[43]

An historical record notes that during the Rebellion of 1837, the 32nd Regiment, while marching to put down an uprising in Windsor, stopped at the school grounds to camp and cook supper and breakfast.[44]

At one point, when a new school was required, money was very scarce, so each family participated by furnishing building materials such as logs and nails. About 1878, the school moved to its final site, north of the intersection on the east side. It was either replaced by a brick building in 1898 or had its exterior brick veneered, according to one source, "to prevent it from being moved again."[45]

The Coyne's Corners Literary and Debating Society held its first meeting at the schoolhouse on January 4, 1907, and folks came from Port Talbot, Wallacetown, and Dutton for the night's topic: "Intemperance has caused more misery to mankind than war." Those in favour of the statement won the argument. The topic for the next meeting, to be held on January 11, was announced: "That the works of art are more universally admired than the works of nature."[46] The Coyne's Corners Farmers Club also met at the school beginning in 1917. In 1939, Reverend Harry Garbutt, a missionary returned from Africa and a former pupil of the school, gave a talk on his work there.[47]

Strangely, no church was associated with Coyne's Corners, although the school was occasionally used by itinerant Methodist ministers. These men would seek out Henry Coyne and his family, as Coyne himself had been a preacher in Ireland and was recognized as a man of learning. Early Methodist services were sometimes held at his home.

The former McGugan Hotel at Coyne's Corners.

Although the intersection was important in pioneer days, the community around it was bypassed by the railways, which had become more important than roads by the second half of the nineteenth century. By 1895, most of the old hotels and shops had become farm dwellings or outhouses. McGugan's Hotel has been moved to the northwest corner, where it is still standing today, owned by the same family, and is now a home. Just to the north, the school also is still standing but now serves as a residence. Henry and Anna Coyne are buried at St. Peter's Cemetery in Tyrconnell.

Largie

The small village of Largie developed around Concession 3 Dunwich (now County Road 9 or Duff Line) and Old Currie Road (now Largie Road). The district was opened for settlement in the 1840s, with primarily Scottish-born immigrants coming to the area. The first pioneer was James Croft, who arrived in 1841. Eventually the usual community services blossomed around the intersection.

In 1846, the small log SS No. 12 Dunwich was built in one day, east of the intersection on the north side of the road. The first teacher was James McDonald, who was paid $10 a month and boarded with local families.[48] A second school went up in 1854 on the southeast corner, across from the present Largie Church. A former student writing in the *Dutton Advance* in 1889 called this school the Largie Academy: "It was built of unhewn logs, was about twenty feet square, eight feet high, had one door, four small windows and a cottage roof." He continued, "The furniture was of the simplest kind. There were rough boards placed along two sides of the building in a beveled position which were used by the large scholars as desks. Long, rough benches, without backs, were used for seats, which is the cause for so many people around Largie having round shoulders."[49] In 1872, yet another school was erected on the west side of Currie Road north of Duff Line. It was probably the meeting place of the Largie Amateur Debating Society as well as of the Largie Literary Society, which existed in the late nineteenth century.

At first, Presbyterian services were held in people's homes, but in summer two open-air meetings were held in Donald Galbraith's woods on the northwest corner of the intersection. Some people walked fifteen or twenty miles to attend. Services were also held in the first log school until construction in 1855, on the east side of the road north of the intersection, of the earliest Duff's Free Presbyterian Church — named after Sir Alexander Duff, a missionary and leader of the Free Church of Scotland in Calcutta, India. He was a powerful speaker and had toured Canada in 1854.[50] However, the place of worship was sometimes nicknamed Currie Road Church[51] or the station at the river.

The building, of timber frame construction, was close to the road and had a low platform across the front so worshippers could alight directly from their wagon or buggy. The cost of construction was $1,000.[52] The land deed stipulated that only a minister who spoke Gaelic and English could preach and that both languages had to be used in every service. An English service was held from 11:00 a.m. to 12:30 p.m., and, after a ten- or fifteen-minute break, Gaelic continued until 3:00 p.m. Use of in the Gaelic language was the general practice until at least 1896. The first regular minister was Reverend Archie McDiarmid, inducted in 1859. The congregation, once part of a union with Chalmers at Cowal, later formed a union with Tait's Corners, which lasted until Tait's joined the United Church of Canada in 1925.[53]

The church continued in use until 1895, when it was closed and torn down. That same year a brick replacement was erected on the southwest corner; one thousand people attended the dedication service.[54] The structure originally had two steeples, but these were removed about 1930 because they were in danger of falling. In 1901, a manse was built just to the south. Also that year, Duff's became the last

Duff's Presbyterian Church, Largie, built 1895. The opening ceremony was so well-attended that even the minister had to do without his chair.

church in the presbytery of London to approve use of an organ during worship; the Presbyterian church had long maintained: "Any element of religious practice that might be deemed Catholic or 'Romish,' including the use of instrumental music and most particularly the unholy instrument of the organ, was ... considered irreligious."[55]

In September 1921, Reverend Charles W. Gordon, moderator of the Presbyterian Church in Canada — who wrote under the pseudonym 'Ralph Connor'[56] — was guest speaker at the anniversary services at Duff's. The crowd was so great that there were people perched right around the pulpit. When Gordon rose to speak, a man took his chair.[57] The church chose to remain Presbyterian in 1925 when others were joining the United Church of Canada.

The Largie cemetery was north of the original church site, located on clay deposits consideral worthless for growing crops. Donald McRae was the first person buried there, in 1850, while the most recent monument is dedicated to Archibald Crawford, who died in 1915. A story is told that one time a young man was walking home past the churchyard late one November night when the moon was up. Suddenly, from within the cemetery, he heard a grinding screech followed by an enormous crash. He then heard footsteps coming in his direction and proceeded to run. A mile down the road he paused for breath but not for long — footsteps were still coming after him at a rapid pace. The young man didn't stop running again until he reached home. The next day he visited neighbours to borrow some equipment and learned that their own son had told the same story at breakfast that morning. He also had approached the graveyard, had heard the crash, and ran. So it had been *his* footsteps the first young man had heard behind him! Investigation showed that the crash had been caused by one of the largest granite stones falling on top of the graveyard fence.[58]

A post office was opened at Largie in 1855 by Neil McEachran. The village had one other postmaster, D. McCallum, before closing temporarily in 1866. The office reopened on January 1, 1868, under Archibald Leitch, and was later run by Hugh McPherson before closing again on August 10, 1871. Once again the facility reopened on February 1, 1873, this time with Allen McPherson as postmaster, before closing for good on May 3, 1884. The post

The churchyard at Largie. A terrible screeching sound coming from this cemetery made a young man run for his life one moonlit night long ago.

office was named after Largie, Kintyre, Scotland, whence many of the settlers hailed. When it was operating, mail was brought in on horseback from Tyrconnell.

Although often the post office was in the home of the postmaster, it was at one time in a general store on the northeast corner of the intersection. The corner also held a blacksmith and carriage shop operated by Allen and Daniel McPherson until 1886, after which Andrew McCallum owned it. Another local business was the cheese factory south of the corners and run by a Mr. McWilliam. A brickyard belonging to the Welch family sat behind the cemetery, and Purdy's sawmill was nearby. Largie also had branches of the Grange and of the Patrons of Industry.[59]

A tavern — variously known as the Auger Hole or Largie House — sat north of the village and served as a gambling and drinking den from about 1850 to 1880. Originally, it seems to have been north of Celtic Line. Owen Crossley was the first owner, followed by Edward Milligan, Mr. Scrolley, and Mr. McCallum. Apparently this establishment became quite rowdy at times. One story tells about a time when the tavern fell behind in taxes and the sheriff went out from St. Thomas with papers to seize the property. He travelled as far as Wallacetown and decided to stay the night there, but word reached Largie to expect him the next morning, and a group met at the tavern to take charge of the situation. They literally moved the pub to the other side of the road during the night; when the sheriff arrived, the pub was suddenly on Concession 2, not Concession 1 as stated in his documents. Apparently he never returned, and the tavern stayed in business.[60] However, perhaps the pub had to move because so many locals hated the rowdy behaviour at the first location.

Above: Largie School, constructed 1872, is now a family home.

Left: A road sign on Dunborough Road points the way to a village no longer there.

The Auger Hole was a favourite stopping place for farmers from Ekfrid Township who were hauling their grain to Tyrconnell on Lake Erie. The pub remained busy as long as this activity continued. But in the 1850s, when the railway was built through Ekfrid Township, Glencoe was founded, and Ekfrid farmers no longer needed to travel to Tyrconnell to sell their produce or purchase provisions. Afterwards the tavern catered mostly to local farmers popping in for a drink, and it closed about 1880. It ultimately became a pigpen for a nearby farmer.

Largie did not last as long as some of the township's other hamlets. It has already been stated that the post office closed for good in 1884, after which local residents went to Campbellton for their mail. The store probably also shut down about this time. Fire destroyed the blacksmith and carriage shop about 1895. W.A. Ostrander moved the cheese factory to Dutton about 1888 and set about enlarging and modernizing his enterprise, but a few years later it too burned down and was never replaced. The last blacksmith shop went up in flames in the early 1960s. The school closed and was bought by Mac Gordon for $1,140.[61] Now all that remains of Largie is the church, its manse and cemetery, and the school on the next road to the east.

Port Talbot

The earliest European settlement in Elgin County was founded on Lake Erie, just off Fingal Line. This was the home of Colonel Thomas Talbot and his first group of settlers, the heart of the Talbot Settlement. Little remains today of what was once an important halfway point between Detroit and Niagara and a supply base for settlements developing farther inland.

Thomas Talbot, born at Malahide Castle, near Dublin, Ireland, on July 19, 1771, was the fourth son in a wealthy family of twelve children. His parents were Sir Richard Talbot and his wife, Margaret O'Reilly. Thomas received a commission as ensign in the 66th Foot in 1783 when he was only eleven years of age. By September 27, he was a lieutenant. In his youth he was a friend of Arthur Wellesley, later Duke of Wellington, who was also of Irish background. Talbot

Portrait of Colonel Thomas Talbot, *n.d., James B. Wandesford, artist. Watercolour on card, 67.3 cm x 49.5 cm.*

Collection of McIntosh Gallery, The University of Western Ontario. Gift of Judge Talbot MacBeth, 1941.

Courtesy of Western Archives.

Talbot's residence, "Malahide," was named after his ancestral home in Ireland. The section on the left, built 1822, was his original home. His nephew, Richard Airey, added the portion on the right in 1848.

was stationed at Quebec in 1790, rose rapidly through the ranks, and by 1791 had been promoted to captain. Five years later he was a major and by 1796 a lieutenant-colonel. He had found favour with Lieutenant-Governor John Graves Simcoe and, beginning in February 1792, was his private secretary.

Thomas Talbot left Simcoe's staff in 1794 and was fighting the French in Holland five years later. On Christmas Day, 1800, he sold his commission; no one seems to know why — perhaps disappointment in love, thwarted political ambitions, or failure to advance in the military — or maybe he simply wished to assist in the development of Upper Canada.[62]

Simcoe wrote to Lord Hobart, secretary of state for war and the colonies, recommending Talbot as a good man to have involved in the settlement of Upper Canada. Accordingly, Talbot received a grant of 5,000 acres on Lake Erie. For every settler he located on a fifty-acre lot, he received two hundred acres, so that by 1837 he had amassed 650,000 acres in twenty-eight townships, 98,700 acres of which were cleared and settled with 50,000 settlers.[63] That year the executive council of Upper Canada transferred control of the Talbot Settlement to the Crown Lands Commission.

On May 21, 1803, Talbot stepped ashore near the mouth of a stream that became known as Talbot Creek. This site would later become a Lake Erie port, also bearing his name. Grabbing an axe from an attendant, he cut down the first tree himself. His companion was a discharged soldier named George Crane, who became one of Dunwich's first settlers. At the time of their arrival, the closest European settlement was at Long Point on Lake Erie, some sixty miles to the east. Talbot immediately set about building himself a home on the summit of the hill overlooking the mouth of the creek.

Much has been written about Talbot's first settlers, most of whom scattered themselves along the lakeshore to the west of Port Talbot in the direction of Tyrconnell. One was George Crane, who in 1806 built his home at Plum Point, a peninsula jutting into the lake between Port Talbot and Tyrconnell. Others included Charles Scarlet, Mark Chase, John Crawford, James Witton, John Davis, and Daniel Kingsland, who may have settled west of Port Talbot along the lakeshore. Another early arrival was Colonel Mahlon Burwell, who in 1809 set up a home at Port Talbot in the valley below Talbot's home and lived there with his wife, children, and parents (see Burwell's Corners). Other pioneers farther west included Colonel Leslie Patterson, John Pearce, Stephen Backus, and Mary Storey, with her son Walter.

In 1804, Talbot hired James Witton, a carpenter, to construct a number of buildings for him, and it was probably that same year that a gristmill went up. By 1808 or 1809, there was a sawmill as well. After Talbot recommended him as registrar of what was then Middlesex County, Mahlon Burwell erected a bridge over the creek and incorporated the first registry office within his home. An 1813 map drawn by Lewis Burwell, Mahlon's brother, shows many industries: sawmill, gristmill, flax mill, warehouses, cooper shop, blacksmith shop, several poultry houses, and a distillery.[64] A horse mill had a treadmill with five long arms to which horses or oxen were attached to operate the saw, but this may have been used mainly to cut firewood.

Talbot, as commander of the local militia, put up two forts at Port Talbot, one on a narrow peninsula, the other on Mt. Pisgah, north of the port. This second blockhouse was meant to serve as a retreat position should an invasion come by water. Invaders did indeed come, but always by land, thus effectively cutting off this intended refuge.

The Americans and their Aboriginal allies were well aware of the strategic importance of Port Talbot and attacked it regularly. There seem to have been four main assaults during the War of 1812, all taking place in 1814. On May 20, Talbot was away at Long Point, and Andrew Westbrook, a traitor from Delaware, a community near London, swept down on the community and took Captain Gilman Wilson and miller Walter Galbraith prisoner at one of the mills. Colonel Patterson, apparently in charge of the settlement while Talbot was away, was taken prisoner at the blacksmith shop. He escaped from the mill; the captors feared he would spread the alarm and forced Wilson and Patterson to take oaths of neutrality, and released them under threat of burning their houses. Since they couldn't find Talbot anyway, the invaders retreated with all the loot they could take with them.[65]

On July 20, a force of about two hundred Americans appeared and burned crops. In August, another raiding party came. Its numbers included several Aboriginals, along with white men dressed as Natives — "Blue-Eyed Indians," who were Americans and Canadian traitors. Their goal was to plunder Talbot's property and capture him; he was in his house but escaped. He was seen by the "Indians," who levelled their rifles at him and are said to have fired three times without hitting him. As he was surrounded by sheep and in plain clothes, he looked somewhat like a workman. The captured Patterson is reputed to have told the rebels, "He's only the man that tends the sheep."[66] They lowered their rifles and then proceeded west, thinking to overtake Talbot who was presumed to have headed in that direction. On this same occasion, Colonel Burwell was captured by the American force. He was in bed with a fever but dragged off and taken as a prisoner of war to Chilicothe, Ohio. His wife, Sarah, was helping him escape out the back door when a heavy coughing spell betrayed his presence.[67]

Andrew Westbrook returned to Port Talbot on September 9 and burned the gristmill, sawmill, and several houses and barns, including those of Mahlon Burwell. Talbot's flour supplies were destroyed, and all his cattle killed. This is said to have been the last raid of the war.[68]

Other stories have been told about the wartime attacks, none of which can be traced to a specific date or occasion. These may be fact or only legends embellished during the retelling, but they certainly are entertaining. Talbot is said to have disguised himself as a woman on more than one occasion to escape capture. One tale tells of how he was seen in his kitchen dressed in women's clothing and explaining to attackers that he was only the cook.[69] Another recounts how Sarah Burwell, Mahlon's wife, looked out her window one day and saw a strange person wearing a sunbonnet walking quickly to her house. The figure leaped up the front steps, and Mrs. Burwell opened the front door for her. Imagine her surprise when she recognized Talbot's face. "Hide me, Mrs. Burwell!" he said. "The Americans are trying to capture me." She helped him climb up the chimney onto a ledge. A loud knocking was heard at the door, and Mrs. Burwell went to open it. An American soldier demanded to know if she'd seen Talbot. She supposedly replied, "No, indeed, no doubt he is in one of the ravines which surround our house, or one of the settlers may have taken him to St. Thomas." The Americans searched without luck and left.[70]

Mrs. Patterson, the colonel's wife, is said to have outwitted an attempted plunder one day when she wore a pea jacket in which she concealed many of Talbot's belongings. When her attackers swung their weapons over her, she dared them to hurt her. Apparently they chose not do so but instead set fire to the buildings and punctured all the water vessels. Colonel Patterson is said to have patched the vessels with clay and carried water from the creek to douse the flames.[71] Captain Wilson also escaped capture by hiding in an oven.[72] On another occasion, Talbot allegedly slipped out one door of his home just as a Commander Walker and his men were entering at another.[73] If all these tales are true, life at Port Talbot was very exciting during the War of 1812! However, often the attackers did not get much loot, as supplies were hidden in the woods and no settler would go to the storage spot unless there was a storm that would obliterate any tracks.

After the war was over, there was more opportunity for the fledgling settlement to grow — and yet it did not. There may be several reasons for this. The gristmill was never rebuilt, possibly because compensation for war losses did not come until the 1820s.[74] There may not have been a mill again until 1881 when Talbot Macbeth built a sawmill near the mouth of the creek; he shipped lumber out from a dock he built himself. Also, the harbour at Port Talbot might have been of poor quality. But Talbot himself was impressed with the site he had chosen. He had written to Simcoe on July 17, 1803, describing Port Talbot as "a fine Bay where vessels can come to anchor with safety within 20 yards of the shore"; he continues to describe Talbot Creek: "on my left flank a beautiful river flows and empties itself into the Bay navigable for large boats for 3 miles and for a short distance a sufficient depth for vessels, but ... shut up with sand when the wind blows strong into the Bay ... by a trifling expense the mouth could be kept open enough to admit vessels."[75]

Not everyone was so impressed. Charles Askin, a militia captain who was with General Isaac Brock on his Detroit campaign from July 24 to September 12, 1812, describes the harbour: "there was such an appearance of a storm that McCaul who sailed our boat thought it advisable to put into Port Talbot distance 7 miles from Kettle Creek, this was a very bad port for our boat for we could not get her into the creek and had to haul her up the beach here we remained all day."[76] Eventually, there was a warehouse at the port where wheat was bought and shipped. However, as there was no dock until Talbot Macbeth built one, a vessel would have to come as near to the land as possible and wheat would be sent out on flat boats. No one seems to have thought it was worth the "trifling expense" to keep the creek free from silt, and as the century progressed, it is likely ships would have become too large to navigate Talbot Creek anyway.

After Colonel Burwell returned from being held prisoner in Ohio during the war, he and his family moved inland to Burwell's Corners. Postal archives list him as postmaster at Port Talbot in 1832, but he was actually living up at his corners, the real location of the post office. His next known successor took over in 1853 — John Clark, probably the man mentioned at Burwell's Corners. Next, George Macbeth held the position until the facility closed September 1, 1870. The office reopened on November 11, 1875, under Andrew Lunn and was later operated by John Brown and Thomas Lunn before shutting down for good on October 1, 1914. The *Dutton Advance* commented, "The rapid advances of present day conveniences is removing one by one the old landmarks. The last to disappear is the Port Talbot post office, which, with the advent of rural delivery, closed its doors on the first of the month, and henceforth will live only in memory."[77]

Although the village did not experience much growth following the War of 1812, Thomas Talbot spent most of the rest of his life there. His correspondence always started with "Port Talbot" and the date.[78] He built himself a new, larger home in 1833, which he called the "Hermitage," but which is usually referred to as "Malahide," after his ancestral home in Ireland. It sat on the west side of the mouth of the creek. Anna Jameson, author of *Winter Studies and Summer Rambles in Canada*, visited him in July 1837. She mentions he had sixteen acres of orchard and describes his home as "long," with a covered porch running along the south side.[79] Talbot's faithful servant, Jeffrey Hunter, lived beside the lake just west of his house and was his nearest neighbour.

As Talbot never married, he had no heir. He decided to introduce his sister Margaret's son to the pioneer way of life. Accordingly, his nephew Julius Airey came out in 1833 but took little interest in life in Canada. He returned to England in 1841 to become a lawyer. In 1846, Talbot again wrote to England, this time to Julius's older brother, Richard, and invited him to give up a military career and come out to Canada. Richard Airey came with his wife and family and stayed with the Burwells while an addition was added to Talbot's house. Unfortunately, Airey could not get along with his uncle. Perhaps Talbot was too cantankerous; perhaps his nephew too anxious to take charge. By the time he took actual control of the Port Talbot lands in 1850, he and Talbot were hardly speaking.[80]

Now in his seventy-ninth year, Thomas Talbot, along with his assistant, George Macbeth, sailed back to England. Two years later, Richard Airey and family returned to England and rented Talbot's old estate to John Sanders. When Talbot returned to Canada in 1852 he found his heir gone and strangers in his old home. However, when Macbeth married one of Sanders's daughters and purchased a home in London, Talbot went there to live with them. He died in Macbeth's house in London on February 6, 1853, just a few months short of the fiftieth anniversary of his founding of Port Talbot.[81] He was buried in the Anglican churchyard at Tyrconnell, just west of Port Talbot.

The Macbeth family inherited Talbot's estate. Unused estate land was divided into farms, and the population of the area increased. The presence of more children meant that a local school was needed. Macbeth donated land in 1862 for a school on what is now Erin Line,

Courtesy of Elgin County Archives R6SSb1B2F29.

Port Talbot in the 1940s.

north of Fingal Line. By 1910, however, the section required two schools, and another went up on the north side of Fingal Line, just east of Talbot Creek. In 1946, when there were only nine students at both schools, the one on Erin Line closed and all students were sent to the south one, which closed in 1965.

In 1925, Talbot's old estate was acquired by a group of Detroit businessmen who planned to build a luxury resort, complete with private dock, hotel, bridle paths, ski and toboggan slides, and a golf course. However, the Depression ended these plans, and the property passed from hand to hand until the 1990s, when the land fell once again into the hands of developers. The derelict house was demolished in 1997 — a sad ending for the home that was the heart of Elgin's earliest settlement.

This roadside monument to the Talbot Settlement was placed at Port Talbot by the Historic Sites and Monuments Board of Canada in 1926.

There is another aspect to the history of Port Talbot, one that applies as well to the many ports and communities along the shores of Lake Erie. During the mid-nineteenth century, when many Blacks were fleeing the oppression of slavery in the southern United States, a number of them escaped by crossing the lake using whatever flotation devices they could find. Robin Winks, in his book, *Blacks in Canada*, published in 1971, mentions that fugitive Blacks landed at Ports Talbot, Burwell, and Stanley. There are many stories yet to be told.[82]

Commemorative celebrations for Port Talbot and the Talbot Settlement have taken place over the years. On May 21, 1903, Talbot Anniversary Day was held in St. Thomas, and the Elgin Historical and Scientific Institute organized a banquet at the Grand Central Hotel. The Historic Sites and Monuments Board of Canada placed a cairn by the roadside in 1926 that still stands today. A sign points to the "Port Talbot Estate," although Talbot's home itself is gone. Otherwise, there is little to remind us of Talbot and his efforts.

Tyrconnell

Just down Lakeview Line from Port Talbot was one of Elgin County's most successful early communities.

Having one of the best natural harbours on the north shore of Lake Erie, Tyrconnell was a busy port in pioneer days, but a combination of factors would turn it into Elgin's best example of a ghost town.

Tyrconnell's pioneer settlers arrived at Port Talbot and moved west to take up their properties. Included in this group were George Crane, Colonel Leslie Patterson, John Pearce, Mary Storey, and Stephen Backus, along with their families. Other arrivals chose to stay closer to Port Talbot. George Crane, who had travelled with Talbot himself, remained with him a few years and then moved on to Plum Point, a peninsula between Port Talbot and Tyrconnell.

These newcomers were originally from Ireland, emigrants who had gone first to the United States about 1800. Wishing to remain under the British flag, however, they decided to relocate to Upper Canada. Pearce, Patterson, Storey, and their families, plus a hired man — thirteen people in all — set out in a large open boat from Erie, Pennsylvania, and rowed around the eastern end of Lake Erie via Buffalo, keeping near the shore. Young Walter Storey, Mary's son, walked around by land, driving their cattle before him. They would go ashore at night, build a fire, and stretch canvas on poles to sleep under — except for the hired man, who slept in the boat. One night their vessel was badly damaged in a storm. In order to make repairs, they travelled a few miles and found a piece of an old boat that had been abandoned along the shore. They burned it to obtain its nails, used these to repair their own craft, and resumed their journey. It took them a month to reach Port Talbot.[83]

They were met by Colonel Talbot himself on July 14, 1809. He was especially pleased to see they had with them looms and spinning wheels — items badly needed to make woollen and linen goods. Talbot reportedly went down to the beach, welcomed them, and carried one little boy, William, only four years old, up the hill in his arms.[84]

Most of these early settlers were related to each other. Patterson was married to Lydia Backus of Vermont. Mary Storey, a widow, was Patterson's sister, as was Frances, wife of John Pearce. Stephen Backus arrived the following year, 1810, and soon married Anne Storey, Mary's daughter. Patterson became deputy to Registrar

RESIDENCE of JOHN PEARCE.
BROKEN LOT Nº 10 CONCESSION 10 TOWNSHIP OF DUNWICH.
COUNTY OF ELGIN ONT.

Illustrated Historical Atlas of the County of Elgin.

The home of John Pearce and family near Tyrconnell in 1877. Pearces still reside on this land and have given their name to the nearby provincial park.

Three postmarks show Tyrconnell's history from Upper Canada to Canada West to Ontario. Note that sometimes the name was spelled with only one "l."

Mahlon Burwell and, ultimately, a justice of the peace, authorized to swear affidavits, write documents, and perform marriages.

Since most pioneer settlers were Irish, the community became known as "Little Ireland." Once a village started to develop on lot 9, it became known as "No. 9," and its creek as "No. 9 Creek." Later, when a post office opened, the name became Tyrconnell. The name comes probably from a relative of Talbot's, Sir Richard Talbot, Earl of Tyrconnell, who lived in the seventeenth century.[85]

Newcomers had to go to Colonel Burwell's office for their mail. However, post office records show that the first official postmaster at Tyrconnell was Joseph Patterson, who seemingly held the position from about 1837 to April 7, 1842. On this date Leslie Patterson took over. The official in 1853 was Thomas Coyne, a son of Henry Coyne (see Coyne's Corners). Later incumbents were James Blackwood, Joseph Mitchell, Peter Cameron, Meredith Conn, Samuel Harris, Reverend John Sanderson, John O'Brien, Atkinson Conn, Adella Payson, Mrs. William Page, George Bexton, and James Page.

The first industries to take root in Tyrconnell were mills. These services were greatly needed; settlers were tired of grinding their grain on hand mills and using a whipsaw to cut all their lumber. Their nearest mill was at Long Point, some sixty miles to the east, and the journey was by boat, hardly a convenience. The first local facility was built in 1817, when Buller and Haynes constructed a gristmill on the lower section of No. 9 Creek. Their venture was not successful, however, and they sold it to George Henry. A Mr. Colby erected a sawmill about half a mile up the creek; he too became discouraged and decided there was not enough water to turn the waterwheel. He also sold out to George Henry. Henry built his own gristmill in the 1820s, downstream from Colby's, and would later also put up a sawmill there, as well as constructing a carding machine in the vicinity.

Another early mill owner, noted in the records, was Frank Siddle, who may have bought Henry's business or started out on his own.

In the early 1820s, Absalom Shade built a warehouse at the lake.[86] He then hired an American named Wheaton Hewitt to keep a store there, while Shade provided the goods to be sold. Hewitt also constructed an ashery, bought black salts from settlers, and made potash and pearl ash.[87] It seems, however, that his business soon failed: "an American named Hewitt made a stir in Tyrconnell about 1825 and led the people to expect great things from him, but he failed the next year and left the country."[88]

In 1826, Archibald McIntyre erected a distillery below Henry's mill, and in 1830 a Mr. Steele built another. Whisky was in great demand in pioneer days. McIntyre is said to have bartered five quarts of whisky for one bushel of corn and one-and-a half gallons for a bushel of rye.[89] Early Tyrconnell also had tanneries, possibly as early as the 1820s. One was founded by George Henry's brother, Philip, who eventually sold it to a Mr. Ladd in 1834. Ladd hired Timothy Moore to operate the enterprise for him.

A general store was opened in 1830 by James Hamilton and John Warren — presumably the men who built the first mill at Selbourne (see Selbourne). Mr. Groundike bought them out in 1833, then sold out to the Ladd brothers, one of them possibly the Ladd who purchased the tannery. The store was next operated by James and Thomas Coyne, sons of Henry Coyne of Coyne's Corners.

The first school at Tyrconnell was kept in John Pearce's house in 1822. The teacher was Thomas Gardiner, brother of Anna Coyne (see Coyne's Corners) and of Singleton Gardiner, who founded Cashmere in Mosa Township, Middlesex County.[90] Thomas was not truly a schoolteacher, but, as he was an educated man and was spending the winter with John and Fanny Pearce, he seemed to be the best candidate. Fanny supposedly vacated her kitchen — a room of sixteen square feet — so it could become a schoolroom. Children as young as six are described as walking three miles through the woods to attend.[91] Classes were later held in a log building owned by Thomas Gardiner. It was a private institution, and parents paid tuition quarterly. There were no trustees, and the people who sent the most children hired the teacher.

A story persists that the school was surrounded by fields of either flax (or hemp) and that Gardiner used the children as free labour to harvest the crop. Allegedly, when reading, writing, and arithmetic had been gone over, the youngsters were sent to pull flax until noon. Then their timetables were repeated again, and next they pulled flax until four o'clock. And as if this weren't enough, Mrs. Gardiner was said to have the older girls do her churning for her in their home in another part of the building.[92]

Parents may have tired of paying the Gardiners to teach their children to pull flax and churn butter. By 1824, John Miles Farlane was keeping a school in his log home to the east of Tyrconnell. A large willow tree stood beside his home for many years, said to have been planted by the teacher over the grave of one of his children. Mrs. Farlane helped to make ends meet by taking in boarders, one being Hercules Burwell, Mahlon's son.[93] This institution also proved to be unpopular, as it was not centrally located. The next school was built in 1824 at Stephen Backus's home, closer to Tyrconnell.

Ink in those days was made from maple bark and copperas — a ferrous sulphate crystal, a highly versatile iron chemical used to make printers' ink. To keep it from freezing overnight during the winter, whisky was added to the mixture. Goose quills served as pens.[94] The Bible was the source for learning both spelling and reading, and children were expected to spell even the most difficult words correctly.

When the Backus school fell into decay, Meredith Conn, Sr., organized a bee to build a log replacement in 1835 on the corner of his property east of Tyrconnell. The first school within the community itself came into being in 1847, in the back room of a house owned by Enoch Clarke. No steps led up to the room, so children had to climb up into it. Pigs ran under the building and mingled their "voices" with those of the youngsters. There were no desks, only slab seats. Not even the teacher, Jane Best, had a desk, only a chair.[95] Finally, a real schoolhouse, SS No. 2 Dunwich, was built on a road leading into the village and was in place by 1848. A new school may have gone up in 1856, on the property of James Blackwell, south of St. George Street.[96] About eight years later, a larger one was constructed west of the village; this was enlarged to two rooms in 1881, when there were

St. Peter's Anglican Church, Tyrconnell. One of the oldest places of worship in southwestern Ontario, its construction began in 1827, with settlers taking on the work themselves. The man on the ladder is doing repairs in summer 2007.

seventy-five children in attendance. Ultimately, in 1907, a red-brick building was erected, designed to seat sixty students.

The need for a church was felt quite early. Services were held at Colonel Patterson's or Colonel Talbot's home before a place of worship went up. St. Peter's Anglican was begun in 1827, after Mary Storey donated ten acres of her land for a church and burial ground. The edifice was constructed of local oak, with families such as the Pattersons, Backuses, Storeys, and Pearces providing labour and materials. Patterson went by boat to Buffalo to purchase the glass, putty, lead, and oil. Stephen Backus put the shingles on. John Pearce finished the interior by plastering the walls and ceiling and making seats, a reading desk, and a pulpit. When the first service was held on October 28, the structure was not yet finished, so a carpenter's bench served as a pulpit and planks resting on blocks of wood as pews. The belfry and tower would not be added for another eighteen years; in 1845, they were built for a bell donated by the Earl of Galloway.[97] Charlotte Simcoe, a daughter of John Graves and Elizabeth Simcoe, had donated a silver communion service in 1844.[98] A stained-glass window is dedicated to Mary Storey, her daughter Anne, and her son-in-law Stephen Backus.

The cemetery is across the road on the south side. It was set aside even earlier than the church, dating from 1825. The first burial may have been that of Leslie Patterson, Jr., who died at age four in March of that year. However, the first entry in the church registry is that of Matthew Stuart, who passed away on November 9 at the age of thirty.

A Methodist congregation, the first one in Dunwich Township, developed at Tyrconnell as well. Meredith Conn, Sr., led a class, which was quite popular until, in his own words, "the Millerites preached in the neighbourhood and caused great excitement by their sophistry and delusions, alleging that the end of all things in this world ... was at hand."[99] Everyone but Conn, his immediate family, and two or three other people joined these Millerites, effectively ending Conn's class for several years. Yet a frame Tyrconnell Methodist Church was built in the summer of 1855, and a cemetery was laid out in 1870. Meredith Conn, Sr., was buried there; he died at ninety-nine years of age in 1889. This church became part of the United Church of Canada in 1925.

The most important figure in mid-nineteenth-century Tyrconnell was James Blackwood, previously of St. Thomas. He purchased the land on which the village was laid out from George Macbeth, Colonel Talbot's heir, in 1853. He surveyed the land into village lots and sold $16,000 worth. He then spent $10,000 building a house with fine grounds for himself.[100] He constructed in 1855 a general store, and in 1856 a warehouse, whence in 1856 he shipped the grain he purchased from local farmers. However, he was already in debt before he came to Tyrconnell, and never did regain his fortune. A recession in 1856, following the end of the Crimean War, further impeded his business. The lots fell back into the hands of George Macbeth when Blackwood could not gain clear title to the land.

Yet between 1853 and 1860, many tradesmen and labourers bought lots at Tyrconnell. The *Canada Directory* of 1857 lists three carpenters, two blacksmiths, one builder, one hotelkeeper, one tailor, one cooper, two storekeepers (including James Blackwood, who was also postmaster), two carriage makers, one miller, one cabinetmaker, one harness maker, two shoemakers, the village schoolteacher, and two ministers. The population was listed as five hundred people.[101] A real village had developed and would continue to grow — for a while.

It has been said that Tyrconnell's lack of success was caused by Colonel Talbot. Frequently, Talbot was accused of refusing to grant title deeds to businessmen. He disliked industrial development, it is reported, because it made settlers less self-sufficient. He thought all women should be able to spin and weave and that all men should be able to shoe their own horses and do the simple metal work needed on their farms. This would explain his refusal to give land in Tyrconnell to a man who wanted to build a blacksmith shop.[102] One set of businessmen, Buller and Haynes, are said to have moved on after having a disagreement with Talbot over the land their

Map of the village of Tyrconnell in 1877.

Illustrated Historical Atlas of the County of Elgin.

80

mill was built on.[103] Another partnership, Henry and Moore, also did so, allegedly because Colonel Talbot would not grant title deeds.[104]

Talbot's antiquated ideas may have impeded the early development of the village but cannot explain its eventual demise. Long after he was dead, *Armstrong's Directory* in 1872 still mentions four hundred residents: "This village is favourably located for manufacturing purposes; the large Creek affords much hydraulic power." It then describes Joseph Mitchell's Flour and Grist Mills as "capable of grinding and dressing 400 bushels daily" and the tannery run by William S. Morden, where "10,000 sides of harness and leather, kip and calf skins are turned out annually." There is a "good school" with average attendance of one hundred. Both churches are holding two services a day. The Tyrconnel [sic] Hotel is "in good style for public convenience and comfort"; the Globe is also "worthy of public patronage." The business community is as large as it was in the 1850s.[105] Yet the 1877 Page's *Illustrated Historical Atlas* describes it differently, "Tyrconnell to-day is only a small post village, important commercially only from the large amount of grain there bought and shipped by Meredith Conn, Esq."[106] In the 1880s, the addition to the school was removed because enrolment had declined; one room was enough.

Meredith Conn, Jr., was one of Tyrconnell's most important businessmen.

What happened to Tyrconnell? One problem was its failure to develop its good natural harbour into a better port. In the early days, all produce shipped from the village had to be transferred to larger boats by scow, as there was no dock for larger boats. In 1853, the Tyrconnell Wharf and Harbour Company was formed to build a pier.

The directors were Peter Gow, Joseph Mitchell, Thomas Coyne, John Hidden, and Robert Gow. This enterprise failed, perhaps because of the recession of 1856, which also had created financial difficulties for James Blackwood.

In April 1861, the Dunwich Pier Company was created, with John Pearce, Peter Gow, John McKillop, Meredith Conn, Jr., and James Black as directors. The firm completed a 500-foot pier at Tyrconnell. The amount of grain shipped from it by Meredith Conn, Jr., and other people varied from 25,000 bushels to 75,000 bushels per year.[107] The pier was thirty feet across — wide enough so that a team of horses could turn around at the end and still leave plenty of space to pile products. The pier was well-guarded at the time of the Fenian Raids in the mid-1860s, as it was considered important enough to be a possible landing place for invaders from the United States.[108]

If Tyrconnell had built a pier and developed its harbour at an earlier date, it might have grown as large as Port Stanley, Port Burwell, or any other large north-shore port. By the time Tyrconnell businessmen became organized, it was too late. In the 1850s, the railway age began. Gradually, use of the rail lines to ship produce and wood increased, and farmers no longer needed to ship their grain out by boat at Tyrconnell. Unlike ports that had developed earlier, Tyrconnell had never diversified its industries or even developed a large fishing industry. As well, other larger ports on Lake Erie, such as Burwell and Stanley, were also serviced by the railway, giving them an extra edge for development. Once no longer being used for shipping, Tyrconnell had nothing to fall back on when the railway began to dominate the shipping trade. The community became merely an outlet for produce from the surrounding countryside.

By 1890, the pier was in use so rarely that it became unsafe. That year Meredith Conn, Jr., asked the township of Dunwich to take over ownership and maintenance of the pier, but it refused.[109] Two horses drowned in the lake in 1892 when they fell through the pier.[110] By 1895 a nearby warehouse was still standing, but local writer Walter Pearce reported that no more business was being done.[111]

An oil field near Tyrconnell dated back to 1866, when the Dunwich Oil Company started to look for potential pumping sites.[112] Interest in petroleum was high as people watched fortunes being made in nearby Lambton County at such places as Petrolia. Dunwich was never a bonanza site, although some wells were still being pumped intermittently in 1950. Perhaps, if the wells had produced a greater volume of oil, Tyrconnell might have developed into a more prominent community.

By the early twentieth century, the only people who visited Tyrconnell were lone fishermen or picnic parties. The post office closed April 30, 1913. The United Church place of worship closed in the late 1920s, when there were too few adherents to carry on as a congregation. The remaining members began attending church in Wallacetown, and the building became a chicken house.

During Prohibition in the 1920s and early 1930s, Tyrconnell's main industry seems to have been rum-running. It was an out-of-the-way spot, unlike Port Stanley and Port Burwell, where cargo was under constant scrutiny by both customs and police officers. At various times a long, low motor launch would anchor offshore at night and wait for a truck to arrive. Then men in the truck would place their cargo in the lagoon under an old iron bridge, dip their headlights, and drive away. A boat would then row to shore and pick it up. Eventually this launch was captured near Port Burwell by customs officials.[113]

The school closed. A reunion was held on August 13, 1966, when a Mr. Addlington of Victoria, British Columbia, won the prize for coming the farthest distance to attend.[114] The building was afterwards sold to Bob and Isabelle Davis of Detroit, who planned to turn it into a summer home. However, a person driving along Lakeview Line today would not see any indication of this school.

The fact that progress bypassed this area means that much of the heritage has been preserved, by chance. Driving westward along Lakeview Line today one can find a great many reminders of this early Elgin community. Just west of Plum Point on the north, or right, side of the road is a white cottage that once belonged to Meredith Conn, Sr., and family. This regency cottage still has its original floors and entranceway dating from its construction about 1828. Two doors down on the north side is the Stephen Backus homestead, built about 1830. After going beyond a newer residence on the south side, the road next passes the home of Colonel Leslie Patterson — the large white house set well back in the trees on the south side at the curve of the road. Built in 1827 and called "Sunnyside," it is the oldest house in Dunwich Township. Next comes St. Peter's — one of southwestern Ontario's oldest churches — with its adjoining cemetery on the south side of the road. This graveyard is the final resting place of most of the players in this story: Colonel Thomas Talbot, his servant Jeffrey Hunter, Henry and Anna Coyne (see Coyne's Corners), Colonel Leslie and Lydia Patterson and children, Mary Storey and son Walter, Stephen and Anne Backus, John and Frances Pearce, and George and Isabella Crane. A plaque was dedicated by Lieutenant-Governor Henry Jackman in 1996.

The grave of Colonel Thomas Talbot (right) at St. Peter's Cemetery. The plaque to the left was unveiled in 2005 by the Elgin Historical Society.

On May 21, 1961, a sign on the church across the road was unveiled to honour Sergeant Ellis Sifton, VC, of nearby Wallacetown, who died at Vimy Ridge in April 1917. The same day a dedication ceremony took place at Colonel Talbot's restored gravesite; Talbot's estate at nearby Port Talbot was open that day, and about 1,000 people toured it.[115] In 2005, a new plaque was placed beside his grave by the Elgin Historical Society.

Next on the left is the John E. Pearce Provincial Park, on land donated by John E. Pearce, a descendant. A marble plaque was unveiled the day the park opened on August 17, 1959. By continuing

The Backus-Page house, built 1850, was the first brick home in Dunwich Township. Now restored by the Tyrconnell Heritage Society, it is open to the public.

The village hall at Tyrconnell. At one time this community had a population of five hundred people.

over a hill to the west, one comes on the right side of the road to a Georgian, red-brick, eleven-room home — "Lakeview." This house was built in 1850 by Andrew Backus, son of Stephen and Anne, and the first brick house in Dunwich Township. It was later owned by the Page family. In 1968, the Ontario government bought the Backus-Page House. In 1998, it gave a fifty-year lease to the Tyrconnell Heritage Society, with the condition that the society preserve the house, which still has its original front door, windows, and floors. To the west of this on the south side of the road is the homestead where John Pearce settled in 1809, still owned by the family.

By proceeding farther west, one approaches some of Tyrconnell's side streets, George Street and Hill Street. To the south on George Street, on the east side, is Tyrconnell's old hall. Near the end of Hill Street on the south side is a house with a columned porch; this was once a Lodge Hall. Still farther west is Erie Street, the former main intersection of Tyrconnell. It ends down at the lake, where two supports for a bridge that once crossed No. 9 Creek are still to be seen. At the far end of the former village is Tyrconnell Cemetery, the final resting place of Meredith Conn, Sr., and his wife, Catherine.

Chapter Four

Township of Malahide

This township, christened in 1810, takes its name from Malahide Castle, Colonel Thomas Talbot's ancestral home near Dublin, Ireland. No doubt he named the township himself. The origin of the name is controversial, but Malahide may mean something like "Ide's hilltop" in old Irish.[1] Most of the early settlers were immigrants directly from England, Scotland, and Ireland, but some had migrated there from Nova Scotia. In January 1998, Malahide Township, South Dorchester Township, and the village of Springfield joined to form the municipality of Malahide.

Carter's Corners

A Baptist church and school once stood at the corner of Talbot Line and Carter Road. The Carters owned the surrounding land, and it is for them the intersection and road are named. The church was dismantled over forty years ago, and the school is gone as well.

Devonport (Davenport)

Several years before Port Bruce was founded along the shores of Lake Erie, another village was situated just to the west of it. Located on Dexter Line, Devonport was about where Waneeta Beach is now.

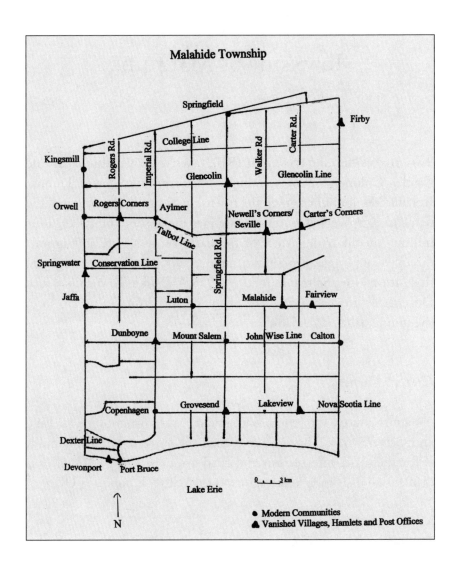

Malahide Township

Colonel John Hale owned much of the land around what is now Port Bruce, having been given a Crown grant of 2,000 acres in 1817.[2] After he died in 1838, his estate passed to his son Edward. Even though the mouth of Catfish Creek was recognized as an obvious place to found a port, the Hales do not seem to have been interested in development of their property. They refused to sell any of the land at the creek mouth to build on, and it remained the neglected reserve of absentee landowners for some time. Perhaps the family was waiting for land values to increase.

Therefore, when Henry Dalley of Devonshire, England, arrived about 1833 it was necessary for him to purchase a farm on the hill about half a mile west of the present Port Bruce harbour. As the creek mouth was inaccessible to him, he visualized cutting a channel from Catfish Creek to his own, more westerly site, thus enabling him to build a bustling port and village around his own estate.

And an estate it was! Dalley had plenty of money, and soon after arriving he had a beautiful house built, complete with an English-style landscape garden. And adding to the splendour was a racetrack, laid out on a large nearby field. It has been said that he kept servants, a coach, and a coachman.[3]

Dalley (and probably other people) poured money into the new development. Streets were surveyed, lots were sold, and a hotel was established, along with a general store, tailor shop, post office (which opened in 1842), warehouses, and a blacksmith. Edward and Sarah Mihell operated the store. Most of the buildings were on the south side of the road, although there were a few on the north, mainly along the brow of the hill. Dalley bought grain, wool, and other goods on credit or by barter and shipped them to foreign markets. He barged them out to lake ships, as the mouth of the creek was too full of silt to allow any large vessels to enter. Buoyed by optimism, in 1835 he also had a railway route surveyed from London to Devonport by Daniel Hanvey of St. Thomas. Dalley named his new village Devonport after his home county in England, but over time the spelling changed to Davenport — the official post office spelling. I use the spelling that Dalley himself had intended.

In 1835, Henry Dalley wrote to Lieutenant-Governor Sir John Colborne; he called Port Stanley "a miserable abortion and never can be a harbour, there being no room in the creek for any vessel to lay sheltered from the winds, and the waters so shallow that heavily laden schooners cannot enter, even after such immense sums of from $20 to $30,000 have been expended ... continually filling up its mouth with sand tho' an excavating machine has been daily employed every summer season from the commencement of piers being made." He preferred his own community: "all intelligent skillful men acquainted with the local situation of the lake and shores agree in the superiority possessed by the Catfish Creek and its being the easiest port made ... This new town called Devonport is just formed which must from its pleasant advantageous, admirable situation, soon become a place of equal importance to any in these parts."[4]

It seems unlikely Dalley expected Colborne to do anything disadvantageous to Port Stanley, but he may have been hoping for some sort of government support for his own enterprise. None came. His channel was not cut, nor the requested railway line built.

The Hale family finally sold two lots at the mouth of Catfish Creek to Lindley Moore and Amasa Lewis, who built a warehouse and a pier extending 400 feet into Lake Erie. They named their new harbour Port Bruce after James Bruce, Earl of Elgin, governor general of Canada. On September 10, 1851, a gathering took place to celebrate construction of the pier and warehouse, along with the naming of the port. A picnic dinner was held at 3:00 p.m. in the warehouse, with about one hundred guests raising a toast to "James, Earl of Elgin." Another toast was raised to Port Bruce itself — "May her prosperity never cease until she competes successfully with any port on the lake." The company then raised yet another to Moore and Lewis and planted a pine tree to commemorate the day.[5] From then on, large amounts of timber, grain, and staves were brought daily by the wagon load to be shipped out to Buffalo and other destinations.

There had been minor development at Port Bruce before this date. There were other grain buyers there besides Lewis and Moore, namely Andrew Hume, Thomas Thompson, and Stephen Davis. Shipping had been active at Port Bruce before the warehouse was built in 1851. Since roads were generally in terrible shape, teams of men unloaded their cargoes on Catfish Creek, quite a distance from the port, and the cargoes were then scowed down to a waiting ship.

A postcard shows the harbour at Port Bruce, c. 1909. Here at the mouth of Catfish Creek, where it empties into Lake Erie, a pier was built. During the navigable season, the port was busy shipping out timber and grain. The nearby community of Devonport could not compete with the harbour facilities at Port Bruce.

A news article from the *St. Thomas Dispatch* on December 14, 1854, says, "Port Bruce is a beautiful and thriving village" — not a likely observation if it had been founded only three years earlier.

This competition explains why Devonport seems to have slid into a decline in the 1840s. The post office closed in 1846, and Mihell shut down his store in 1847. But Moore and Lewis's development seems to have sounded the village's death knell. Dalley and his associates could not compete as more and more goods were being shipped directly out of Port Bruce. He overextended his credit and was ruined financially. Gradually Devonport's buildings literally were moved down the hill and re-established in the new village. Dalley's own little community was practically gone by the 1860s.

Only a few structures were standing in 1877; Page's *Illustrated Historical Atlas* of that year stated, "The ruins of the village are there now ... Davenport was a place of great promise, but small fulfillment." Dalley was still living nearby: the atlas continues "The Dalley farm now invites the second look from the passer by, and with its hedges and beautiful trees of cedar and chestnut seems to require only money to make it like one of the 'Stately homes of England.'"[6] It is said that Dalley returned to England later and then went to Australia, where he amassed a fortune.[7] One would like to think he finally met with success elsewhere.

In 1921, Lorenzo Banghart bought fifteen acres of land that comprised most of the original Devonport. He developed it into a fine summer resort, Davenport Heights. A Mr. Wilson bought the property in 1926 and renamed it Ormond Beach in honour of his daughter Ormond. In 1947, a group of Londoners purchased the place and called it Wingate Lodge and Country Club, after General Orde Charles Wingate (1903–44), a British intelligence officer in Palestine in the 1930s and a commander in Burma during the Second World War.[8] There is still a Wingate Road to the west of Port Bruce leading into some cottage properties. In the 1930s, this area was referred to as "Devonport Hill." Waneeta Beach is just to the east of this area today. But the land on which Dalley's home and village stood has probably eroded into the lake, along with the original road.

Amasa Lewis's house — "Whitehall" — is the one high on the hill in the centre of Port Bruce, built in 1860 for his wife, Amy. [9] Today, as Port Bruce Manor, it has large, high-ceilinged rooms, several fireplaces, and a fine winding set of stairs leading to a cupola on top of the house with a "Captain's walk." There are streets in the village named Amasa and Lindley — but nothing else to remind us of Devonport's past.

Dunboyne

The hamlet of Dunboyne was located at the corner of Imperial Road and Concession 3 Malahide (now Calton Line). While never large, it had some of the essential services needed by pioneer farming families — church, school, post office, blacksmith, shoemaker, and cheese factory.

The first name for the community was Nickerson's Corners, after the Levi Nickerson family, which owned land on the southwest corner. The hamlet became Dunboyne on August 1, 1881, when Joseph Norman opened a post office there. The original Dunboyne was a small village northwest of Dublin, Ireland, now part of that Irish capital's suburban sprawl. The name means "Baethan's fort" in old Irish.[10] Nickerson is said to have used his influence to name the post office after Governor General Lord Dufferin's residence in Ireland.[11]

An early school was set up some time before 1855; the exact date is not known. The brick SS No. 5 Malahide, later Dunboyne School, was built in 1872 on land on the southwest corner, bought from Levi Nickerson. At one point it had an enrolment of 115 pupils.

On June 22, 1855, a community meeting was held at the earlier school to discuss building a union meeting hall to be shared by the Methodist Episcopal, Methodist New Connexion, Freewill Baptist, Presbyterian, and Particular Baptist congregations. The church was dedicated February 23, 1857, and became the Seminary Chapel, or the Silver Creek Union Meeting House. Records show that a John Smith received $3 for building fires, cutting wood, and lighting lamps at the church from November 21, 1864, to May 15, 1865.[12] However, friction developed among the denominations, and the Methodists withdrew, deciding to build a sanctuary of their own. In 1910, the old church was replaced by the present red-brick one, set about one hundred yards to the west of the previous site. The cornerstone for the new church was laid on April 28, 1910, after which the large crowd went to the cheese factory for a "splendid supper."[13]

When Joseph Norman opened the post office in 1881, he operated it in his shoemaker's shop, and continued to maintain it until he died on February 22, 1918. Later postmasters were John S. Crosby, Mrs. S.E. Crosby, and Edna Kent. By 1910, the post office was on the southwest corner of the intersection, while the Dunboyne Cheese and Butter Factory, founded by William Bothwell, was to the north of the intersection, on the east side of the road. After many years of ownership by the Bothwells, the factory was sold to John Wardell but burned down sometime after 1910. Some years later there was a service station on the southwest corner. An H. Percy was one of the last people to operate the garage.

In the early days, there was also a blacksmith shop in the vicinity, run by a Mr. Hossack. The first bicycle in the district and possibly in

Elgin County was built there by Perry Doolittle and Robert Anger in the later nineteenth century.[14] Doolittle, born near Luton, graduated in medicine from Trinity College, Toronto, but automobiles became his obsession, and he was the first doctor in Toronto to make his rounds by car. Doolittle founded the Ontario Motor League, and when it became part of the Canadian Automobile Association (CAA), he went on to become its president, serving 1920–33. He was an advocate for the building of the Trans Canada Highway and drove most of the planned route and mapped it himself, driving a Model T Ford from Vancouver to Halifax.[15]

Malahide United Church, Dunboyne, as it looks today.

Dunboyne also had its clubs and organizations. A Dunboyne Patrons of Industry Club was in existence in the 1890s, and a Christian Endeavour Society was also organized at about that time. Today, the hamlet's main building is the former Methodist church, now Malahide United, on the northeast side of the intersection.

Firby
See Bayham Township.

Glencolin

Glencolin was created by the railway in the nineteenth century and developed into a typical small Elgin village that provided several services for local farmers and their families. It was located at Concession 8 (now Glencolin Line) and Springfield Road, where the Grand Trunk intersected with the roads.

A church was the first building, as was the case at so many other communities. In 1864 John and Lydia Bowen gave half an acre of their land on the southeast corner of Glencolin Line and Walker Line for a Methodist chapel. While not right at the main intersection but down Glencolin Line to the east, the church was always an integral part of this community. When the original structure burned in 1899, a new red-brick one was built in 1900 that became Trinity Methodist Church. At that time there were forty or more families that belonged — a sizeable congregation.

A frame school was built on a plot of land donated by Samuel T. Young, southwest of Glencolin Line and Springfield Road. A brick edifice replaced the original structure about 1872.

Before 1875, the intersection was known as Reilley's Corners. Samuel Young became the first postmaster on February 1, 1875, and opened a post office on his property, north of the railway tracks on the west side of the road. An immigrant to Canada West (now Ontario) in 1856, he changed the name to Glen Colin in honour of his home in Scotland. At first, it was necessary for him to go to Springfield to pick up the mail, but later the railway installed a mail hook at Glen Colin; a bag would be left beside the tracks, and as the train went slowly through the intersection, the bag would be picked up by a hook and another bag left in its place. Young operated his post office until he passed away June 12, 1908, after which his widow took over. Eventually the name was combined into one word — Glencolin.

Other businesses were soon to open. John Chambers may have had the first sawmill in the district, set on the northeast corner of the Walker Road intersection. John M. Staley had a saw and shingle mill down the road to the east as well, but not as far as Walker Road. At its peak in the late nineteenth century, Glencolin also had a hotel, store, post office, church and school, and a blacksmith shop operated by Peter Coyle. The hotel was on the southeast corner, and the blacksmith shop on the other side. The population of the area is considered to have been about one hundred at its maximum.

The post office was closed July 22, 1911, once the system of rural mail delivery was introduced, and other businesses gradually closed as well. The store and post office were torn down in the early 1900s, but local resident Kathleen Oatman remembers digging up old medicine bottles on the site about mid-century. Trinity Church was demolished about ten years ago, and a new Mennonite church was built nearby. The railway tracks remain and are still used, but no train has stopped here for about fifty years. Today, newer houses are clustered around the intersection.

Grovesend

Most of this lakeshore community was located at the corner of "Cod Fish Lane" (Concession 1, later County Road 42, and now Nova Scotia Line) and Springfield Line, but part stretched along Nova Scotia Line to the east. It was in many ways the typical small community of the nineteenth century, but its history is in many ways more macabre than most.

A school was built on land belonging to Gilbert Wrong, probably east of the intersection. It may have appeared as early as 1830, but there are no records be-fore 1847. Wrong's daughter Elizabeth was a teacher there that year, starting out with just four pupils. She also taught sewing to a class of eight little girls.[16] It is noted that on the day of Confederation, July 1, 1867, a school picnic was held there, with a brass

Grovesend School, built c. 1870.

Courtesy of Elgin County Archives C10Sh4B2F6.

band in attendance, and a local boy recited E.H. Dewart's poem "An Ode to Canada" for the occasion.[17] About 1870, the first school became a carpenter's shop, and a brick replacement was built to the west, on the northeast corner of the intersection.

Two adept Grovesend children were George McKinnon Wrong and Horatio Nelson Chute. Wrong (1860–1948) became professor of history at the University of Toronto and author of many books.[18] Chute (1847–1928) was teaching mathematics and physics in the high school at Ann Arbor, Michigan, in 1873. His career flourished and he too published many books, including a manual of practical physics.[19]

Early services in the neighbourhood were held in the first school. Then, in 1863, John Markle donated land for a Wesleyan Methodist church on the northeast corner of the intersection, just east of where the new school would be built. The church was replaced by another structure in the 1880s. One teacher named George Peacock loved music and introduced singing as a subject at the school. When the trustees decided not to renew his employment and hired someone else, Peacock was encouraged by parents to carry on in the church.[20]

In the 1870s, Grovesend had about seventy-five residents; in contrast nearby Port Bruce still had only fifty. Grovesend boasted a general store, post office, blacksmith, wagon-making shop, carpentry shop, grist- and sawmills, church, school, and cheese factory. Mail

arrived tri-weekly. The post office had opened February 6, 1852, under Joseph W. Stone. Later postmasters were W.B. Lyon, William Bothwell, Mary A. Bothwell, W.E. Godfrey, Mary Tobin, Mary Thomas, Gordon L. Nelson, Mrs. John P. Tedford, and Lewis Hawkinson. The name for the community

Courtesy of Elgin County Archives C10SB4B2F6.

Grovesend Methodist Church stood on land donated by John Markle in 1863.

was chosen because the intersection marked the end of a long stretch of beautiful trees.[21]

The mills were probably east of the main intersection at Stalter's Gully, east of Sawmill Road, where a little stream crosses under the highway today. William Northrupp had the stream harnessed by a dam to power his mill, which he sold in 1837 to John Saxton and Ed Griffin. The gully received its name when Charles Stalter took over the mills in later years. The wooden bridge that ran over this stream was often replaced as the gap widened. After the span built in 1916 collapsed, people had to detour via the next concession to go east or west. A new steel bridge was constructed in 1922.

Just west of Stalter's Gully, on the south side of the road, stood a frame hotel — the Halfway House (Grovesend was about half way between Port Bruce and Port Burwell) — owned by Samuel Tedford. He also started a cobbler's shop nearby. Grovesend also had a Patrons of Industry lodge, and, according to an Aylmer newspaper item written in 1892 by the Grovesend correspondent, may have been developing a library: "A few of the grateful people of Grovesend went to Aylmer on Saturday to select some reading material for the rest of us: we will be better enlightened hereafter."[22]

Yet this idyllic-sounding little village was more than once the site of tragedy. For one thing, there were many shipwrecks off the coast, and bodies that washed ashore were sometimes buried at the cemeteries at Grovesend and Lakeview. Often the unidentified victims were interred in unmarked graves.

The Grovesend neighbourhood was the site of an attempted robbery on May 8, 1865, when Dan Mann, John Sharp, and James Dyke arrived to rob John Haggan, who lived just east of Stalter's Gully. Haggan was thought to have lots of money on hand, as he had just returned from Ingersoll, where he had been selling the cheese produced at the Grovesend Cheese Factory. The men first stole three horses from a man named Elijah Saxton for their getaway. One horse threw its rider off and returned home. The thrown man was taken on one of the other horses, and all three made off over the fields.

When the would-be robbers arrived at the home of Haggan's neighbours, the Franklins, a bulldog was awakened. Its barking alerted the residents, and lights started appearing in windows. The men abandoned their original plan and continued west, until they stopped and knocked on the door of Walter and Catherine Chute, their home being west of Sawmill Road. They told the Chutes they had broken their wagon and needed help to fix it. When Walter opened the door, they attacked him and tied up both him and his wife. The two children, Horatio (of future physics fame), aged seventeen, and Ensley, ten, were asleep. The robbers demanded Chute's money at gunpoint and took $15 from him.

Horatio was awakened by the noise downstairs, jumped out of a window, and sped to the next farm to the east, where his uncle, Richard Chute, lived. Richard and his brother-in-law Isaac Smith came running back with guns. When the robbers saw help was arriving, Mann and Sharp ran to the barn and stole one of Walter Chute's horses. Isaac Smith exchanged shots with the men as they galloped away. (The barn door, peppered with shots, was a showplace for years when visitors came.) Richard Chute and James Dyke played a hide-and-seek game around the house for some time. Finally, they located one another, and both fired at once. Dyke's shot hit a pump handle, but Chute's shot went home. Dyke was found groaning near a fence. Thinking he was dying, he turned Queen's evidence and told the whole story. Because of his confession he went free, but Sharp and Mann, who were eventually rounded up after a few days, received prison sentences.[23]

This story pales in comparison to the sensational Marshall Piggott murder case. Piggott was a local resident who disappeared on November 17, 1884. A body, bound with rope and with a broken skull, washed up on the west shore of Long Point later that winter. It was buried by the local lighthouse keeper, W.E. Dickenson, who notified authorities. An advertisement was placed in newspapers describing the body and was seen by Marshall's brother John who lived in Bay City, Michigan. He and his mother, Lavina, went to Long Point to view the remains. Lavina thought the socks were ones she had knitted for him; brother John identified the boots as Marshall's and recognized a mark on the right big toe. One of Marshall's friends was Havelock Smith, who suddenly came up with the story that Marshall had sold him his farm for $1,000 the day before he disappeared.

Detective John Wilson Murray, a well-known provincial investigator considered to be Ontario's first official detective, was brought on the case. Some facts were soon discovered: Havelock Smith had rented a rowboat from a Mr. Pankhurst of Port Bruce at the time of the disappearance and didn't return it until December 3, 1884. The rental was secret, as Smith's brother knew nothing about it. Smith claimed he rented the boat to get fish from nets along the shore, but there were no nets at that time of year and no one saw him out on the lake. Evidence suggested Piggott had died of a severe blow to the head. The heavy iron lid of Ensley Chute's sugaring kettle was missing, and it was thought it might have been used as a weight to hold down the body. Then a neighbour stated he had seen Smith the day of Marshall's disappearance wearing wet pants and carrying a gun.

However, the most damaging evidence was a note for $13; the evidence suggested that Smith, who was in financial difficulties, had borrowed $13 from Piggott. Smith then changed the sum of $13, originally written on the note, to $1,300, the approximate value of Piggott's farm. Smith had apparently also hired Ensley Chute to search the registry office to determine Piggott's financial situation and to check for certain if he had a deed for his farm. The note was dated the day after Piggott disappeared, and the signature was thought to have been forged. The prosecution believed Piggott was inveigled to the gully to help launch the boat, and while busy, was struck with a heavy, blunt instrument that smashed his skull. Based on this evidence, Smith and another man, Arthur Telford, were arrested for murder and taken to the St. Thomas Jail.

The trial, much publicized, began Tuesday, November 24, 1885. The main argument of the defence was that positive identification of the body was impossible as it had been in the lake for some time and was badly decomposed. The first jury was deadlocked. A second trial took place in September 1886, at which time Smith was acquitted and released. Seemingly, the jury did not want to convict in a capital-punishment trial without overwhelming evidence. Havelock Smith afterwards moved to the United States.[24]

A ghost story exists about a young girl who drowned herself at Stalter's Gully because her parents would not allow her to marry the man she loved. After her parents, neighbours, and hired help searched for her all day, they found her body in the stream. Her body was placed on the rope-strung riser of her bed, and everyone went down to the sitting room to wait until morning. During the night, there was a creaking noise in the bedroom, but upon investigation there was nothing wrong. Then the family noticed the bedroom window was open, even though someone had closed it before leaving. They closed it again, but both the window and the bedroom door were opened by an invisible hand once more. This alarmed everyone so much that one of the men propped himself against the door to keep it closed. The door flew open anyway, flinging him across the room. After the body was removed, these strange events ceased.

Afterwards, a man's figure started appearing periodically in the area west of Stalter's Gully. He stood in the middle of the road not far from the Halfway House and frightened many lone drivers and horses.[25] One wonders if he was the girl's unsuitable lover.

Grovesend Cemetery is one of the few reminders of the former village. However, even most of the grave markers have been removed.

Like other small villages, Grovesend disappeared in the early twentieth century. It was not on the railway, nor was it a port. It had nothing to keep it going in the age of the automobile. Harvey and Bruce Barr bought the church and surrounding property in 1931 and moved the building several hundred feet. They used it at first as a garage and later converted it to a home. The old burial ground was partially moved, some of its markers being taken to Aylmer Cemetery. Grovesend post office closed August 31, 1914. The school, SS No. 2 Malahide, shut in 1966 and has since been torn down. As at so many other places, only a cemetery, on the northeast corner, reminds us of a vanished village.

Lakeview

The village of Lakeview developed on Concession 1 Malahide (now Nova Scotia Line) east of Carter Road.

As with most of these communities, the impetus for development stemmed from the local farmers' need for services.

The first log school was built on the north side of the road about 1822, having been organized by a Mr. Olfred; it would later become the location of the Lakeview post office. A second school was constructed farther down the road to the west, on the other side of Carter Road. A teacher there charged 25¢ per pupil per month[26] in the days before free education. A third school went up in 1851 on the northeast corner of Nova Scotia Line and Carter Road; it was replaced in 1864 by a red-brick one that was used for 102 years as SS No. 3 Malahide.

As in many other places, the first religious services were held at the school. Eventually a Baptist church was founded on the south side of the road, a little west of the original school site, on land donated by the Northrupp family. The frame building, erected in 1842, was known as Malahide Jubilee Church (see Estherville). Its first pastor was Reverend Shook McConnell, who attempted to resign in 1855 but was so popular that his congregation would not hear of his leaving. His resignation was finally accepted in 1876 after twenty-seven years of service.[27]

In 1870, a disagreement occurred among adherents concerning the election of a deacon by ballot. Some members organized a meeting, held at Lakeview Temperance Hall, to form a new congregation — Berean Regular Baptist — and their trustees bought a site to the north on Concession 3.[28] By 1894, the mutual bitterness was gone, since the younger generation was not interested in the dispute of 1870.

That year, the two churches reunited as Lakeshore Calvary Baptist and once again began using the building on Nova Scotia Line. A new home for the congregation was built in 1909, and was renamed Lakeview Baptist the following year.[29]

Lakeview Cemetery developed around the church. Graves there date back as early as 1831, and most of the markers are for the Chute family. Sadly, many of the dead interrred there are shipwreck victims. For example, when the steamer *Northern Indiana* burned and lost twenty crew members, one of the bodies washed ashore and was buried at Lakeview Cemetery. The headstone reads "Sacred to the Memory of Thomas Hutton of Mosbro, County of Derby, England, who drowned in Lake Erie at the burning of the 'Northern Indiana' July 17, 1856, aged 61 years." Then there was the *Erie Wave*, a schooner that sank with eight hands in a storm in 1889. The remains that washed up on shore were also buried there and at Grovesend, many of them in unmarked graves, as their identities were unknown.[30] Interestingly, the Lakeview Sons of Temperance called themselves the "Erie Wave" division.[31]

The village may at one point have been called Arnersville.[32] By the 1880s, it was known as Hobbtown, because a small store had

A view of Lakeview Cemetery, where Thomas Hutton, a shipwreck victim, is buried. His marker on the cement pad is the second from the right.

been opened there in 1882 by Joseph Hobbs. Lake View post office opened July 1, 1884, with Hobbs as postmaster; eventually the two words were joined together to form Lakeview. There is a clear view of Lake Erie from anywhere along the road.

After Hobbs's wife died, he sold the store and post office business in 1896 to Fred McConnell, who ran it for a few years. But in 1900, McConnell moved to Toronto and left all of the operations to his parents, Mr. and Mrs. George McConnell. At that time, there was daily mail delivery from Aylmer.

Lakeview store and post office as it looked when it was run by the McConnells. The structure has been demolished, but the home just to the west is still standing.

A cheese factory in the vicinity may have been called the Nova Scotia Street Cheese Company at one point but was also referred to as Lakeview Cheese and Butter Company. A local sawmill was operated by Ephraim H. Doolittle; he also purchased the blacksmith shop east of the store and ran it for several years before selling it to John Henry Sharp, a man considered to be "one of the world's best blacksmiths."[33]

Life at Lakeview was not all work, however; in the 1890s there was an active football club. The *Aylmer Express* on August 20, 1892, reports a game it played with Calton.

Courtesy of Elgin County Archives C10Sb4B2F6.

Lakeview Cheese Factory. Standing on the ground are Theresse, Gordie, and Alex Herrie. The identity of the man on the wagon is not known.

One of the most important enterprises in the area was the McConnell Nursery, started by Hilliard McConnell. He began with a fruit farm, then broadened into growing shrubs when his son Spencer went into partnership with him. Over time, the family enterprise grew so that by the mid-1950s, the McConnell brand had become a mail-order business with sales across Canada. Its nursery stock was being shipped to major outlets such as Loblaws, A&P, Sears, and K-Mart. It was bought out in 1979 but was at one time a multi-million dollar business, with two hundred employees at Lakeview, Tavistock, and Ostrander, north of Tillsonburg.[34] The site where McConnell's used to be at 52429 Nova Scotia Line is now used by Breck's Bulbs, another bulb company that operates a mail-order catalogue.

Gradually buildings disappeared. The cheese company was gone by 1914. The post office closed that same year on August 14, and Mr. and Mrs. McConnell moved to Aylmer. The school shut down in 1966 and was sold to become a meeting hall; it is now a home at the northeast corner of the intersection. Lakeview Baptist Church was torn down in the autumn of 1980; regrettably, its walls had been vandalized by graffiti. Lakeview Store was still standing on the north side of the road about 1987 but has since been demolished. Lakeview Cemetery is just down the road to the west on the south side. Today, the only other reminder of the hamlet is found in the name, Lakeview Compressor Station, located several kilometres to the west.

Malahide and Fairview

These names appear on maps on the south side of Concession 4 Malahide (now John Wise Line) west of Carter Road. Malahide post office was open from 1908 to 1914, its one and only postmaster being John Davis. A few hundred yards down the road was a Methodist church called Fairview, built in 1870. In 1964, after the congregation dwindled, the building was moved to Richmond to become Richmond United Church's Sunday School.

Newell's Corners and Seville

The intersection of Talbot Line and Walker Road once had a blacksmith shop on the southwest corner operated by John Newell, hence the name. Newell lived there with his wife, Elizabeth, until she passed away in 1870. He died in 1912.

There was a Quaker meeting house on the southeast corner. One day Reverend Caleb Burdick stopped in to Newell's blacksmith shop for a chat. Burdick remarked that he was a little disappointed at the poor attendance at services during the summer months. Newell explained that the reason attendance dropped off was lack of footwear; the poor could afford only one pair of new shoes a year. People were ashamed to worship barefoot so did not go at all. From then on, the minister preached many a sermon in bare feet.[35]

Official records show Seville post office beginning in Bayham Township on August 1, 1880, under Judge H. Baker. This suggests the facility was originally just over the townline. Later postmasters at that location were Mary Baker and Lee Cascaden. The office closed on April 11, 1892, but later reopened in Malahide Township in 1909 on Talbot Line, just east of Newell's Corners. The postmistress was Martha Phelps. Because of the name of the post office, the cemetery associated with the Quaker church became known as Seville Cemetery. There does not seem to be any written explanation for the use of the name Seville, best known for a city in Spain.

Another building in this neighbourhood was the cheese factory near the post office. A Mr. Abell built the plant on his farm on the south side of Talbot Line. It would change hands many times. It was the Seville Cheese and Butter Company in 1932 but became the Welter Cheese Factory at one point. The factory, which was forced to close because of increased competition, stood idle for many years and was torn down in 1944.

Across the street just to the east was a hall built on land purchased from George Baker. The Grange frequently used the hall and after it closed, the group held meetings in the church. The place of worship closed in 1892, and it is likely the remaining Quakers used Dunboyne Union Church for their meetings. Their meeting house stood until the 1940s, when it was dismantled and moved to a nearby farm to serve as a barn.

The cemetery has been preserved by having its markers brought together on a concrete pad. John and Elizabeth Newell are buried there, as are Judge and Mrs. Baker and members of the Abell family.

Rogers Corners

This hamlet was at the corner of Talbot Line and Rogers Road just west of Aylmer. It consisted of an inn, a school, a cheese factory, and a large milling business.

The corners were named after the Rogers family, which owned the southeast corner lot. The earliest business seems to have been the Wayside Inn, on the north side of the road just east of the corners. Possibly built as early as 1811, the inn was operated by Simeon Davis. Its main feature was a large ballroom. It is known to have been still standing at the turn of the twentieth century.

On the northwest corner was a frame school also used for religious services. It is said to have been the first school in Elgin County, built in 1816,[36] and was constructed on the land of Isaac Ostrander. Baptist Deacons Davis and Teeple were the main promoters of this dual-purpose building. By 1916, a brick school was in use at this location, but its date is unknown. The Northwood Cheese Factory once stood north of the corner but was closed because of competition with a company in Aylmer.

The main industry at the intersection was a saw and woollen mill, which Joseph Clutton, Sr., purchased from John Freeman in 1853. Three years later, Joseph turned the business over to his sons, Joseph, Jr., and Samuel. Both of the mills were steam-operated, and the sawmill was capable of producing 200,000 feet of pine a year. An advertisement in the *St. Thomas Home Journal* of 1860 notes that "the Clutton factory was turning out 75 yards of cloth daily including tweeds, satins, and jean flannels with the best of the latest Scotch and English styles — and their demand was three times greater."[37] In 1861, the Clutton mill was the largest in Elgin County, employing fifteen men and women and producing 1,500 yards of cloth a year. A fire destroyed both mills in April 1873. Samuel Clutton, who had bought out Joseph's share of the business, built a new three-storey brick mill within a year at the corner of Water and Queen streets in Aylmer.

Rogers Corners could not have developed successfully when so close to the thriving town of Aylmer, and the corners today are practically one of Aylmer's suburbs.

Springwater

Springwater consisted of mills and a school at the corner of the Malahide-Yarmouth Townline (now Springwater Road) and Conservation Line. The school, SS No. 17 Malahide, is still standing on the southeast corner in the Springwater Conservation Area. The saw- and gristmills, owned by the White family, were also within the conservation area's current borders at one point; two millstones are preserved within the park. Springwater Mills still exist just down the road, on Southdale Line to the west.

CHAPTER FIVE

TOWNSHIP OF SOUTH DORCHESTER

SOUTH DORCHESTER, the smallest township in Elgin County and the only one not on Lake Erie, was created in 1798 as Dorchester Township. It was named after Sir Guy Carleton, Lord Dorchester, governor general of Canada 1786–96, whose title comes from the town of Dorchester in Dorset, England.[1] Originally located entirely within Middlesex County, Dorchester was divided into north and south in 1851, with the southern part being transferred to the newly formed Elgin. Its settlers appear to have been mainly immigrants from England. The township officially no longer exists, for in January 1998 it merged with Malahide Township and the village of Springfield to become part of the municipality of Malahide.

Crossley-Hunter

The intersection of Concession 9 South Dorchester (now Crossley-Hunter Line) and Quarter Road (now Dorchester Road) was never more than the tiniest of hamlets. Yet a great deal is known about its buildings — school, church, and post office.

SS No. 7 South Dorchester was originally a log structure built in 1860 to the west of the Crossley-Hunter corners on the south side of the road. One of the teachers was a Mr. Widmore, who stayed three years and was caretaker as well. At night he slept in a bunk on the wall at the back of the schoolroom.[2] A Sunday School was held there as well. In 1872, a white-brick building went up on George

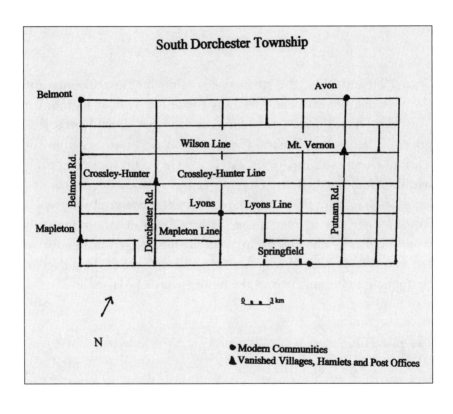

Crossley-Hunter School, SS No. 7 South Dorchester. When the institution closed in 1966, over three hundred former students came to a reunion.

Learn's property on the northwest corner of the Crossley-Hunter intersection. A singing school was held there to while away the long winter evenings; everyone had to bring a candle — the only way to light the room.[3] In 1911, this structure was torn down, and a new red-brick one built on the same site.

James Ballah put up a brick house to the north of these corners that was so large it took three years to complete. Its outstanding feature was a roof on which red slates were arranged in a pattern against a dark grey slate. The design read "Maple Leaf Farm 1885." Soon after, the area became Maple Leaf. A post office of that name opened March 1, 1893, under James Meikle. Regular mail for the settlers was carried on a stagecoach that came to Lyons, southeast of Crossley-Hunter, as part of a route between Aylmer and Dorchester. Meikle would go to Lyons, get the Maple Leaf mail, and take it home. Often mail remained at his house for days before being claimed, and it was common for someone to shout to a neighbour in passing, "Jim Meikle told me to tell you that he has a letter for you."[4]

Maple Leaf did not remain the name of the area for long. The church and vicinity were named after Thomas Crossley and John

Hunter, two men who met as Methodist theology students at Albert College, Belleville. After graduation they kept in touch and formed a team of travelling evangelists. Crossley's sister, Elinor McCreadie, who lived in South Dorchester at the next intersection east of the schoolhouse, suggested he and his partner hold a revival meeting in her neighbourhood. Her husband, Wilson, also encouraged their visit, as he was not only a farmer and tile maker but a local preacher and, for about twenty years, the Sunday School superintendent at Learn's schoolhouse. Ada McCreadie, a sister of Wilson's, was married to Edward Hunter, a brother of John's.[5]

Accordingly, in 1890, Crossley and Hunter preached in the woods just south of the corners. People tied their horses to the trees, hung coal oil lanterns from tree branches, and sat on raised planks. The Aylmer and District Museum has a handbill announcing "Bush Meeting by Revs. Crossley & Hunter in H. Brown's Grove, near Learn's Schoolhouse, 10th Concession South Dorchester, to begin on Friday June 20, 1890, at 8:00 pm and continue nightly for ten days. Three services each Sabbath at 10:30 am, 2:30 pm, and 7:30 pm. The meetings will be undenominational, and all ministers and others are cordially invited to cooperate."

Crossley-Hunter Church, built 1891, is now a home.

The locals were so enthusiastic afterwards that they wanted to build a church. Land was bought from Henry Brown for $50,[6] and a place of worship went up as part of the Lyons Methodist circuit. Presbyterians, Anglicans, and Disciples — probably the Church of Christ Disciples, as this group was also present at nearby Mapleton — assisted with construction and helped to maintain the building. The church was dedicated in 1891 on the southeast corner, and it and the intersection became known as Crossley-Hunter. Reverend James Kennedy was the first minister, but the church was always to be part of a circuit. On its 65th anniversary in 1956, the congregation sang from the hymnals from the 1890 camp meetings.[7] The guest speaker was Dr. Ernest Crossley Hunter of Toronto, a son of Reverend John Hunter.

The village slowly wound down. The life span of the Maple Leaf post office was over and it closed on April 21, 1898. As years passed, members of the church died or moved away to the larger towns and the congregation dwindled until it was no longer possible to maintain. The farewell service was September 13, 1965, when Dr. Hunter related the story of his father's life. The structure was taken over by a Mennonite congregation.

Crossley-Hunter School closed in 1966. A reunion on July 31 of that year attracted more than three hundred former students, some from as far as Detroit. Today, both church and school are homes. Maple Leaf Farm is still standing on the east side of the road north of the intersection, but its roof no longer announces the old post office name.

Mapleton

Mapleton was once a prosperous village at the corner of Concession 11 (now Mapleton Line) and Mapleton-New Sarum Road (later Highway 74, now Belmont Road). It had all the services local farmers could desire at a scenic location on Big Catfish Creek.

The community eventually had three schools. The first one, a log structure, was built after 1842 on the east side of the road, south of the intersection, on land owned by Edwin Culver. One of the early teachers was S.T. Petit, who walked all the way from Hamilton to open the institution. When he arrived, his feet were so swollen his boots had to be *cut* off.[8] Later a second school was erected on the northeast corner of the intersection — a blue-frame building known as the Blue School. It later became a home and was moved to Lyons. The third, also frame, went up in 1870, to the east of the intersection at the foot of the east Mapleton hill; it lasted well into the twentieth century.

In pioneering days, camp meetings were held in the forests in the warmer months and in local homes during winter. In 1843, a young man named Edmund Sheppard from the Church of Christ Disciples in Nottingham, England, came to Canada. He settled in South Dorchester and taught school in Mapleton. He began preaching as well and showed interest in building a church. Baptists of the area assisted him, and the congregation met at his home on January 6, 1850, to start planning. The earliest place of worship was a log cabin with one door and two windows, in which candles were necessary even in daylight.[9] It was the first church in South Dorchester Township.[10] A story has been handed down about a Mrs. McLachlin, who was an invalid confined to a wheelchair; her sons carried her chair to a wagon and took her to church in the back of it.[11]

By 1872, membership had increased, and a larger church was needed, so a white octagonal structure was erected on a Mr. Bentley's property. This church was replaced in 1904 on the same site; the old white brick was used on the inside, but with red brick on the outside. There are two burial places at Mapleton — Mapleton Cemetery, just east of the intersection, and Mapleton Necropolis, farther to the east, surrounding the church.

John Wismer settled east of the site of Mapleton in the late 1820s or early 1830s. He opened a store on the southwest corner of the intersection, operated it for a while, then sold it to William Appleford and built a new store on the northeast corner. John and his brother Stephen went into the general store business together. Over the years the Wismer store changed hands many times, with owners Benjamin Knight, B. Boughner, Thomas McKee, W.A. Baron, the Bray sisters, and Earl McKenzie. After William Appleford left the original store, it was operated by John Doan and Phillip Boughner.

Mapleton Necropolis is the cemetery associated with Mapleton Church of Christ Disciples.

Mapleton was named by Thomas Hughes, a butcher whose home, on the southwest corner to the north of the first store, was surrounded by stately maple trees.[12] When a post office opened September 1, 1856, with Benjamin Wilson as postmaster, it took this name. The office was later operated by Noah Lee, William Appleford, B. Knight, P.N. Boughner, Thomas McKee, William A. Barrows, Darwin Ostrosser, and Maud Bray. Usually, the post office was found in one of the stores.[13] After the railway was built through nearby Kingsmill in 1872, mail was dropped off by train and then taken to Mapleton by horse and cart.

A hotel, built on the northwest corner in 1857, was a popular meeting place for over fifty years. Many of its early clients were men hauling grain over almost impassable mud roads, who would stop there for refreshment and to water their horses.

Ralph Fonger put up the first blacksmith shop; later smiths included Thomas Stanley, Samuel Bancroft, and W. Cloes. Bancroft established a new smithy on the west side of the road.

Mapleton was always known for its cheese factory. The first, situated east of the intersection, was founded by William Appleford in 1859. Though quite small, it was the earliest in the area and probably one of the first in Ontario. Later Appleford set up the Mapleton Cheese Factory, south of the intersection on Catfish Creek. He then bought the Mapleton store and sold the cheese factory to George Mundy. John Brodie was the next to acquire the factory but sold it to Canada Milk Products in 1920, after which time it was torn down.

The next cheese plant was a farmers' co-operative built on the north side of the hamlet in 1932. Harvey Fishback was the founder. This plant ran into trouble financially and closed in 1952 but was revived in 1954 by Fishback, with support from Robert Burgess, Ken Fry, and Ed Bridgeman. In 1975, it burned down but was rebuilt, and the Mapleton Cheese and Butter Company was soon back in business.

In its 1872 edition, *Armstrong's Directory* states that Mapleton has semi-weekly mail and seventy-five residents. William Appleford was postmaster, Wilson Bailey merchant, James F. Brown innkeeper, Thomas Hughes butcher, John Leitch cheesemaker, and George Simmons and James Skiffington were blacksmiths.[14]

Just west of the old tavern, Seth Thompson built a gristmill in the early twentieth century. When it was torn down, W.A. Baron, then a storeowner, constructed a new mill just back of the store on the site of the "Blue School." Keith Drake built and operated a third gristmill on the west side of the village. Mapleton once had a cider mill located to the east of the cemetery. It was owned by W.H. Brown. Each farmer who came to press his apples would operate it with his own horsepower.

Mapleton Women's Institute was founded in 1907. It rapidly expanded its territory and became the Kingsmill-Mapleton Women's Institute the following year. There was also a Mapleton Literary Society established about the time of the First World War.

Like many other small villages, Mapleton did not survive the twentieth century's dependence on the automobile. Travel became faster and easier, and there was little reason for anyone to shop or do business at the village. The post office was closed on February 28, 1914, when rural mail delivery was set up. Earl McKenzie sold the old store on the northeast corner to the Department of Highways in 1956, and the old building was demolished to give drivers a better view while making the curve on Highway 74.

In 1957, the old tavern on the northwest corner, which had become a grocery store, was also moved to help drivers. The building was transferred to the farm of Robert Cline, two miles to the east.

The move had to be delayed until the Mapleton Cheese Factory finished its production for the day, as hydro service was going to be disrupted while the structure passed under the service lines.[15]

The old blacksmith shop had been bought by Percy Drake in 1939 and turned into a garage, which he operated until he died in 1963; then this building too was moved away. The school also closed in 1964 and was torn down in 1974 to make way for a trailer park.

Above: *Today, the Mapleton store is closed and its sign defaced.*

Left: *The former cheese factory is now the Mapleton Taxidermy and Cheese Store. Cheese is still sold here but is no longer made on the premises.*

Today, a drive through Mapleton will lead one past the Mapleton Taxidermy and Cheese Store on the east side of the road, north of the intersection. Cheese is sold on the premises but no longer made there. Across the street on the west side is the most recent Mapleton store, now closed, its sign defaced. Down the road to the east is the original Mapleton Cemetery, founded 1856, on the north side of the road. One must travel quite a distance to the east to find the Mapleton Church of Christ Disciples on the south side of the road, with its accompanying Mapleton Necropolis.

Mt. Vernon

Situated at the corner of Putnam Road and Wilson Line, Mt. Vernon was also known as Mt. Burnham. It consisted of a Methodist church built in the 1860s on the west side of the road to the south and a school, SS No. 8 South Dorchester, on the northeast corner. A more recent school built in 1914 still stands on the northwest corner.

Silver Hill

According to official records, this post office floated between Norfolk and Elgin counties, depending on who was operating it. It opened under Elizabeth Cole in 1851 and closed in 1932 while being operated by Sidney Gordon Armstrong. It appears on a 1910 map[16] on Lyons Line, to the east of the village of Lyons.

CHAPTER SIX

TOWNSHIP OF SOUTHWOLD

CREATED IN 1792, Southwold Township was named for a town in Suffolk county, England; "wold" in old English means a forest.[1] The place in England is a small coastal resort, so it seems an appropriate name for this township on Lake Erie. Many early settlers were immigrants of English, Scottish, and Irish background, but some of the settlers also came from the fledgling United States. The area is now the municipality of Southwold.

Boxall

Boxall is on Boxall Road, south of Scotch Line. It once consisted of a school, church, brickyard, and post office.

The first log school, ultimately known as SS No. 1 Southwold, was beside a deep gully called "Indian Run." Students would go there for nature lessons. The gully was said to be haunted by a faceless ghost that had been appearing just before each gale on the lake every November since the 1850s. But, interestingly, it was never seen after the opening, during the Second World War, of the nearby Fingal Bombing and Gunnery School, which was part of the British Commonwealth Air Training Plan that prepared RCAF non-pilot aircrew for service overseas.[2]

In 1856, the building of a frame structure a bit to the north of the original school cost $700.[3] Its actual location was on the east side

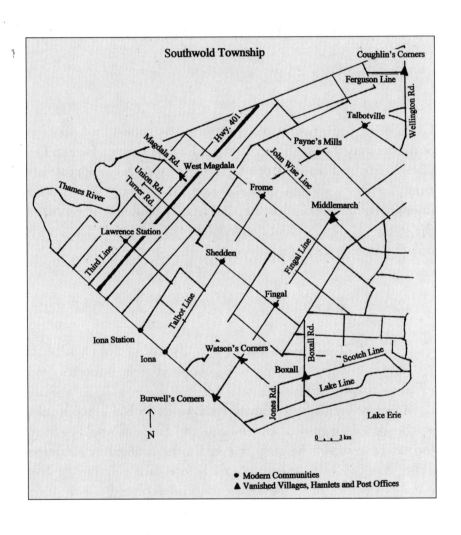

Southwold Township

Coughlin's Corners

Ferguson Line

Wellington Rd.

Talbotville

Payne's Mills

Magdala Rd.

West Magdala

John Wise Line

Union Rd.

Turner Rd.

Frome

Thames River

Middlemarch

Lawrence Station

Fingal Line

Third Line

Shedden

Fingal

Talbot Line

Boxall Rd.

Scotch Line

Iona Station

Watson's Corners

Iona

Boxall

Lake Line

Burwell's Corners

Jones Rd.

Lake Erie

N

0 . . . 3 km

● Modern Communities
▲ Vanished Villages, Hamlets and Post Offices

of Boxall Road not far from Lake Line. In 1889, a new school was constructed of white brick obtained from Donald Baldwin's nearby tile- and brickyard. And yet another brick school was built in 1921; after the post office opened, it became known as Boxall School. The grounds served as the sports centre of the neighbourhood. Baseball was played there every Monday and Thursday night in the warm months, while in winter skating took place at the back of the schoolyard. The property was also used for community events such as picnics, roasts, showers and anniversary parties, dances, and card parties.

The Methodist church was also the centre of much activity. At first local services were held in homes, but ultimately the church was built in 1854 on Lake Line just west of Boxall Road, the land having been donated by Fleming Hunter. The simple structure was frame and almost square, with no steeple, three windows on each side, and one on each side of the door. It seated about one hundred people, men on one side and women on the other. Worship took place at 2:30 p.m., with Sunday School being held afterwards. The first minister was Reverend Francis Chapman, but the congregation was always part of a Methodist circuit with Port Stanley and Dexter. A long shed nearby allowed members to hitch their horses under shelter. Festivals such as strawberry socials and garden parties took place in the shed or on the lawn. As it was the only church in Boxall, Baptists, Presbyterians, and Catholics also used it in the early days.

The closest burial ground was the Hunter Cemetery, sometimes known as Lakeshore Cemetery, about a mile away, where Lake Road connects to Jones Road. The story goes that one day Thomas Hunter and his wife, Amelia, were passing by this site, and Amelia, who was suffering from a fatal illness, told her husband she wished to be buried at that spot. Soon Thomas and his brother Fleming bought the land and set it aside as a cemetery. Amelia died after a lingering illness on November 14, 1859, and was buried on the site she had chosen.[4] Despite this story, there is at least one earlier date on a gravestone, that of James MacKay, who died in 1852. Either the Hunter story is incorrect or James was buried elsewhere first and moved to Hunter Cemetery later.

Another tale states that John Lumley was out riding his horse one day, carrying a switch from the Balm of Gilead tree[5] as a horse whip.

He is said to have thrust it into a fence corner near the cemetery and rode off. The twig took root, grew into a tree, and stood for 150 years across the road from the graveyard. Since he died in 1868, the twig must have rooted well before that time.

Donald Baldwin arrived in the area in 1882, purchased the property of one Hiram Johnson, and started a tile and brick yard. His products were of high quality and thus widely sought after. Thousands of his white bricks went into local homes as well as into the 1889 school. His prolific business is easy to understand when one learns that Baldwin had eight sons to assist him.[6]

This area received its name when Harry Boxall, a native of England, opened a post office on December 1, 1892, on the southwest corner of Scotch Line and Boxall Road. Leonard Else carried mail from Fingal twice a week and later daily. Else rang a bell on his cart to summon the farmers for their mail. After he died in 1909 his brother took on the resposibility for the mail delivery.

This post office remained open only until May 23, 1910, after which time rural mail delivery began from Port Stanley. Harry Boxall went back to farming and died in 1918. It is not clear when the tile yard disappeared. The church membership dwindled as settlers died or moved away, and the building was sold in 1925 to a grandson of Fleming Hunter's, who used it as a stable. The structure was torn down in 1983, as was the Boxall home and post office. The school closed in 1964 and is also gone. Today, a sign says, "Welcome to Boxall."

A sign welcomes today's visitors to the neighbourhood of Boxall. The population figure refers not to an actual village but to the number of people living in this rural area.

Burwell's Corners
See Dunwich Township.

Coughlin's or Townline Corners

The intersection of Wellington Road and Fergusson Line was named after the pioneer Coughlin family. The community had a Methodist, later United, church on its northeast corner and a school on its northwest corner. Townline Corners is a more recent name, created by the fact that Southwold Township is on the west side of the road and Yarmouth Township on the east. The church was recently put up for sale, and the school is still standing but is now a residence.

Above: *This building at Coughlin's Corners proves that even a mid-twentieth century school can be made into an interesting-looking home.*

Left: *Townline United Church was formerly a Methodist church.*

123

Middlemarch

A village developed at the intersection of Fingal Line and John Wise Line, where the Michigan Central railway tracks once ran. In 1900, Middlemarch had a general store, post office, blacksmith shop, wagon maker's shop, hotel, railway station, church, and school, as well as many houses. It is only a ghost of its former self.

One of the earliest settlers was Delbert Smoak, who arrived in 1834.[7] Later, there was a Peter Smoak on the northwest corner of the intersection, and his son Caleb "Kep" Smoak lived in a house nearby. Not surprising, the intersection became known as Smoak's Corners.

George Stanton,
PROPRIETOR DOMINION HOTEL
SMOAK'S CORNERS.
Choice Liquors and Cigars, Good stabling and atter.tive hostlers.

An 1877 advertisement for Stanton's Dominion Hotel. Illustrated Historical Atlas of the County of Elgin. *The official name had actually been Middlemarch since 1876.*

There were various log schools in different locations. One had a very strict teacher named Mr. Phelan; he had only one arm but was known for using it to give out harsh physical punishment.[8] Eventually, a frame school was built near the blacksmith shop. It was replaced in November 1865 by a white-brick school on Amarah Sutton's land, east of the intersection on the north side of the road. A reporter attended this school's official opening for the *Canadian Home Journal* on November 30:

> Wednesday Evening, the 22nd inst., was not one of the most inviting nights imaginable to turn out to a Tea Meeting, but backed by the hearty invitations extended to your Reporter, he started on his journey, through mud and rain, to the new brick school house in No.

14 section, which has lately been erected. Arriving at
our destination, we found the school house brightly
lighted and well warmed, looking doubly welcome,
for the trials of mud and rain endured in reaching
it. While waiting for the arrival of the choir from St.
Thomas, we had an opportunity of looking around
us, and of admiring the very neat room, tastefully
decorated, in which we found ourselves. The school
house was commenced in June of the present year and
was finished and opened at the date of this festival. It
cost about $800, which has been raised by assessment
in the Section; it is a model of convenience. The choir
— consisting of several ladies and gentlemen from St.
Thomas, having arrived, proceedings commenced by
moving John King, Esq., into the chair. After singing
grace, refreshments were served and they were the
best we ever saw at a Tea meeting — we grow hungry
as we reflect. Now came the speaking interspersed
with singing. The chairman in opening the meeting
gave a very able and impressive speech, dwelling upon
the liberal advantages afforded, educationally, in the
present day compared to those he had enjoyed in
that very section in his youth. No gift which a parent
could bestow upon a child ever could equal the gift of
a good education.[9]

A story from the 1870s relates how one of the boys pinned a
squirrel's tail onto the coat of teacher's coat. William Ellison, the
teacher, found out what the students were laughing at and is reported
as giving the boy a "good shaking."[10] This early school was replaced
by a red-brick one built on the same site in 1907.

When a post office opened on December 1, 1875, under an
Englishman named Thomas Hatherley, it took the name Hatherley
in his honour. Fearing that it would be confused with another
Ontario post office, Atherley, officials asked for an alternative. Local
resident Jabel Robinson was reading George Eliot's popular novel
Middlemarch and suggested its title as a possibility.[11] The proposal

was accepted, and the crossroads has officially been Middlemarch since March 1, 1876. Later postmasters included Frank Westlake, Albert Heard, Albert Stinchcombe, and Mabel Stinchcombe.

The front of the Smoaks' farm was divided into lots, and it was on their land that much of the village was built. George Jones constructed a blacksmith shop on one of their lots on the northwest corner; his son John was the next to run the shop. In 1873, it was purchased by Thomas Hatherley, who added a wagon shop to the building. This smithy became a popular place for local schoolboys who would stop on their way home to watch horses being shod. It became a sort of meeting place where men would also stop to catch up on the latest news. Later smiths were John Kent, Frank Westlake, and Albert Stinchcombe, who took over in 1888. Eventually, this shop was moved further north and a general store opened in its place.

Thomas Hatherley came to an unfortunate end. In 1892 he was returning home from St. Thomas in his horse and buggy when he stopped to give two men a ride. The men later claimed that he was thrown out when his cart hit a rut. Hatherley reported someone struck him on the back of the neck. His neck was broken, causing paralysis, and he lived only a few days after the presumed accident.[12]

Middlemarch had other businesses. George Stanton operated the Dominion Hotel on the southeast corner. There was also an old man who sold fish, possibly door-to-door. Perhaps because the smell of the fish was not appealing or perhaps because of his retiring demeanour, he was the butt of practical jokes from neighbourhood boys. One night when he was away, some of them put his wagon on top of his house. When he returned, the fish peddler said he would have the boys arrested if they did not remove it from his roof. The boys tied a rope to the greasy axle, threw the other end to the fisherman, and told him to hold the rope as they pushed the wagon off the other side. Needless to say, it crashed, and the old man was left holding the rope. Seemingly, he left the vicinity shortly afterwards.[13]

One of Middlemarch's most important businessmen was Albert Stinchcombe. He and his wife first came from Lambeth and set up housekeeping in the old schoolhouse, still standing after a new one went up. He operated the general store and for fifty-four years, the post office, on the northwest corner of the intersection. He also ran the blacksmith shop at one time.

When the railway was built through the area, many local farmers worked with their teams to make the roadbed. The wage was $3.50 for a ten-hour day, a good supplement to their farm income.[14] Residents must have had high hopes that Middlemarch would grow. Once the rail line was completed, both a station house and stockyards were constructed. Cattle, salt, and fertilizer were shipped in, and milk, cattle, wheat, sheep, hogs, and sugar beets were shipped out. At one time, four passenger trains a day went through the village, although it was a flag station only. Though already operating a store, post office, and blacksmith shop, Albert Stinchcombe became stationmaster as well.

At some point before 1879, some Bible Christians[15] arrived in the area from Talbotville. They held meetings in the local schools and homes, and set up local accommodation by boarding with residents. Their mission was successful, as Peter Smoak and his son Caleb donated land for a church. John Curtis and John Stubbs teamed the lumber from Lambeth and London, and a Mr. Geary was hired as the builder for $1,000.[16] The place of worship opened June 3, 1879. The first minister was a Reverend Williams, who had been preaching in the school until the church was completed. His circuit stretched from Middlemarch to Talbotville, about four miles away. Williams stayed until 1882, when the congregation became Methodist and a Reverend Cobb took over. The first organ was obtained from Watson's Corners in southwestern Southwold Township. Oil lamps in the church dripped so much that a Mr. Page made little pails to hang under them.[17] In 1907, a tornado caused so much damage on the original building that both ends were blown out. But resilient members rebuilt the same year.

Middlemarch had its clubs and organizations as well. The Grange held its first meeting in the schoolhouse in 1875 with fifteen members in attendance. In 1880, John Curtis donated land for a hall. As it was set in an apple orchard, the hall became known as Apple Grove Grange.[18]

A Women's Institute was organized in February 1918 and became very involved in supporting the community. The organization improved the school's grounds and purchased a radio and a record player for school use, performed Red Cross work during the Great War, sponsored classes and courses in home economics and gardening, and put up historical plaques in the area.[19] In 1928, when the Grange closed its doors, the hall was presented to the Women's Institute by Grange shareholders.

Middlemarch was not one of the railway boom towns that developed in the mid-nineteenth century such as St. Thomas. The railway came late to Middlemarch, and, by the turn of the twentieth century, was not likely to create any more large communities. The station was used mainly for shipping farm produce, and it soon became more convenient and economical to transport beets and other crops by truck. When freight trains eventually stopped running through the community, the station was converted into a garage.

Middlemarch's other buildings became victims of 'progress' as well. When Albert Stinchcombe died in 1944, his wife, Mabel, took over as postmistress and their son, Trevor, continued running the general store. However, the post office closed March 31, 1948, and the area became RR 1, St. Thomas. The church's dwindling congregation held a meeting in 1954 to decide on its future. It chose to close the church at the end of the year, sell the property, and start

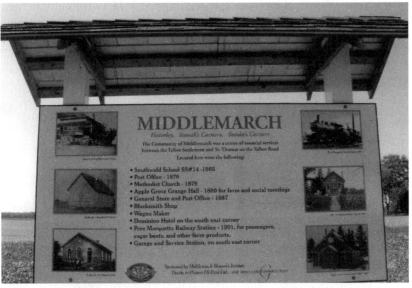

This sign was placed on the southwest corner at Middlemarch by the Women's Institute in 2006. It is a fine tribute to the village's history.

attending Fingal Church. The pulpit, two chairs, and a communion set went to the Iona Christian Fellowship. By 1956, the old structure was being used as a chicken hatchery, but in 1967 it was demolished to make way for a new house. The school closed in 1964. Apple Grove Grange was torn down in 1987. And now even the tracks have been ripped up.

Today, there are still road signs announcing Middlemarch, but few visitors would guess that the crossroads was once a busy railway village. The general store still stands on the northwest corner, having been converted into a home about fifty years ago. In 2006, the Women's Institute placed a historical sign on the southwest corner to commemorate the community.

Watson's Corners

This hamlet was at Talbot Road (now Fingal Line) and Scotch Line. Despite attempts to develop it into something more substantial in the mid-nineteenth century, it remained best known for its church and school.

James Watson and John Barber left Pennsylvania to settle in Upper Canada in 1810. They stayed for two or three months, then returned to the United States. The following year Barber returned, bringing his wife, Hannah. A man named Burgess Swisher came with him. James Watson did not return until 1812, and when he did he settled on the southwest corner of this intersection. David Watson, posssibly a brother, also built on the southeast corner. With two Watsons on the south side of the road, the fledgling settlement became Watson's Corners.

These pioneers had their share of excitement during the War of 1812. In November 1814, some United States army troops came through and camped in the area that later became St. Thomas. There they captured James and David Watson and one Daniel McIntyre but released the men the next morning. However, the army marched along Talbot Road, plundering as it proceeded, stealing wheat along the way to feed their horses. The troops proceeded to John Barber's house and held him prisoner for two days. They are said to have torn the feathers out of a bed, put clothing inside it, and made Barber carry the load.[20]

Watson's Corners School, officially SS No. 11 in later days, was the first school in Southwold Township.[21] In 1816, James Watson donated a one-acre lot, and a log schoolhouse only 20 feet by 18 feet was built on the site in 1818. The earliest teacher was William Hannah, and the initial trustees were John Barber, James Watson, and Colonel Mahlon Burwell, who lived down the road to the west at Burwell's Corners. Hannah taught for two years and boarded with parents of his pupils. He used the New Testament and *Cobb's Spelling Book* as his texts.[22]

About 1820, the school burned down when a log rolled off the fire onto the floor after school hours.[23] From that point on, Ewen Cameron conducted lessons in various houses until 1830, when a new frame structure went up at the same location. The first teacher in the new building was John W. Clark, who served there for two-and-a-half years before dying of cholera.[24] The next instructor was D.C. Spare, who was reputed to have had a bad temper and was prone to throwing a ruler across the room, aimed at a child's head.[25] He was followed by Crowell Wilson, who stayed for about six years. He was a good Latin scholar and was induced to come by Mahlon Burwell, who was looking for someone to teach his sons Latin, which Wilson did in his spare time over the noon hour. For each of the six years of his service, he received one hundred acres of land extra in London Township, Middlesex County.[26]

One of the students at this school was James Watson's grandson, James Craig Watson (1838–80). He attended Watson's Corners School until he was twelve, after which his parents, William and Rebecca, moved to Ann Arbor, Michigan. Young Watson graduated from the University of Michigan at Ann Arbor and became a well-known astronomer, writing several books on the subject. He was a director of the Detroit Observatory and discovered twenty-two asteroids.[27] His sister Kate also went to Watson's Corners School and later graduated in medicine at Ann Arbor.[28]

In 1893, a white-brick school was built on the site of the frame structure. It was very up to date, with separate entrances and washrooms for boys and girls. One teacher, John McLellan, taught there for twenty-nine years around the turn of the century.

Initially, religious meetings held by Freewill Baptists were in local homes or barns. In 1849, an unused church was moved onto the one-acre school lot at Watson's Corners. After fifteen or so years, it was replaced by another church built by Methodists when a member of the Watson family donated land for the purpose on the southeast corner.

In 1817, Richard Williams, a silk manufacturer, sailed from Liverpool and after a voyage of six weeks landed in New York. He and his family then proceeded to York (now Toronto), and, having purchased a yoke of oxen, started for the Talbot Settlement. They reached there after a ten-day journey through forest and swamp. Williams went directly to Colonel Talbot to obtain land. Apparently when he approached Talbot, the colonel asked in his blunt way, "What do you want?" Williams explained he was after property. Talbot is said to have advised him to take a certain lot, which was already occupied, stating that the settler already there was too lazy to till the soil. Williams did as advised and took up land on the northwest corner of Watson's Corners.[29]

For a short time, the intersection of Watson's Corners was called Manchester after Williams's birthplace in England. Several businesses developed there over the years. Truman Waters kept a tavern or inn in the early days. Later, a dry-goods store was operated by Robert Clark and John Mills. Henry Fillmore ran a wool-carding machine and bending factory. At one time, there was a general store with a medicine "factory" at the back, which processed local herbs supplied by Dr. Henry Needham and his son Murray, presumably for medicinal use. As the senior Needham was murdered in St. Thomas in 1872,[30] the herbal production must have been operating before this date. However, there was never a post office, and no official name was ever applied to the intersection. The name Watson's Corners was maintained for the longest period in the lifespan of the settlement.

The church was moved to Fingal about 1887. The school closed in 1964 and was sold to Frank Crabe, who converted it into a home. It has often changed hands but is still standing today on the southwest corner.

Watson's Corners School, SS No. 11 Southwold, has been made into a charming home.

West Magdala

This community was spread out along Concession 3 Southwold (now Third Line) between Turner and Magdala roads. It consisted of a post office, general store, creamery, brickyard, church, and school.

The first crude log school was built before 1850 on the northwest corner of Third Line and Magdala Road. Boys and girls sat on opposite sides of the room on benches facing a long desk attached to the walls. The teacher's desk resembled a cupboard and was conveniently large enough to place a child who misbehaved.[31] By 1860, this log structure was described as decaying and desperately in need of repair. In 1867, the year of Confederation, a new school was built on the same site. In 1912, it was moved across the road to the northeast corner of the intersection, and an extra room added. Officially SS No. 3 Southwold, it was variously West Magdala, Oneida, and McBrides School — "Oneida" because the school was on the road leading to the reserve, and "McBrides" after the name of the nearby church. A Grange Hall operated at West Magdala for a while, and in the earlier part of the nineteenth century, members may have met at the school when they did not have a building of their own. A literary society and a singing school, along with other community-based groups, also used the facility.

The first religious services were held in both English and Gaelic in the log school and in the home of Donald Turner. John A. Turner donated land for a Presbyterian place of worship near the school, on the southeast corner of Third Line and Union Road. Neil McKillop named the church after a great Scottish divine, Reverend Peter McBride.[32] The dedication ceremony, held in June 1876, was presided over by Reverend Dr. George Sutherland.

A post office opened July 1, 1869, with Donald Turner as postmaster. He was the only person ever to run the office, which was located in a log cabin on his property on the west side of Magdala Road, north of the Third Line. Turner also operated a general store. A Mr. Lynn usually brought the mail from Fingal, but neighbours would carry letters with them if they just happened to be in Fingal. By 1881 mail was arriving three times a week. The gross revenue for this office never exceeded $63 per year.[33]

The reason for the hamlet's name is unknown. The name tends to be pronounced with the accent on the second syllable by today's residents. In the Bible, Magdala was a small village in Galilee, which may have been the birthplace or home of Mary Magdalene.[34]

The home of Donald Turner, postmaster at West Magdala. The post office was in a nearby log cabin, now demolished.

The creamery was on the south section of Samuel Lynn's farm on the northeast corner of Turner Road and Third Line. It became the West Magdala Creamery. Warren Warner founded the business in 1871, but four years later he sold it to Robert Cranston, who operated it until 1922. Andrew O. Imlay was the next owner. The other significant business in the neighbourhood was a brickyard.

The post office was closed on November 30, 1899. The Presbyterian church joined with Chalmers Presbyterian, Cowal, in 1900, and today a modern bungalow sits on its site. Andrew Imlay operated the creamery until 1951, when he had to close it due to ill health. Some years before it was torn down in 1963, it had been partially burned. The school closed and became a home, which is still standing on the northeast corner, but barely recognizable as a school. Donald Turner's brick home still stands on the west side of Magdala Road north of Third Line, although the log post office has long been torn down.

CHAPTER SEVEN

TOWNSHIP OF YARMOUTH

SURVEYED IN 1792, Yarmouth became part of the new Elgin County upon its inception in 1851. There are two Yarmouths in England, one on the coast of Norfolk and one on the Isle of Wight. It seems likely that this township was named after the Norfolk town, since it is close to the boundary of Suffolk, and other Elgin townships took their names from this area. Yarmouth is Elgin's most populated township, home to the county seat, St. Thomas. Many of the early settlers were United Empire Loyalists or families who emigrated somewhat later from the United States. Most were of English, Scottish, or Irish descent. In January 1998, Yarmouth Township, Port Stanley, and Belmont joined to form the municipality of Central Elgin.

Adrian or Odell

A post office and train station once existed on the Canadian Pacific Railway line near the corner of Yarmouth Centre Road and Ferguson Line. The Adrian post office was in operation from March 16, 1908, until September 1, 1913. The mail for the hamlet arrived by train. Over the five-year span, the only postmasters were John Porter and Norman Porter. The name Odell seems to have also been attached to this area, in recognition of the pioneer Odell family of Westminster and Yarmouth townships.[1]

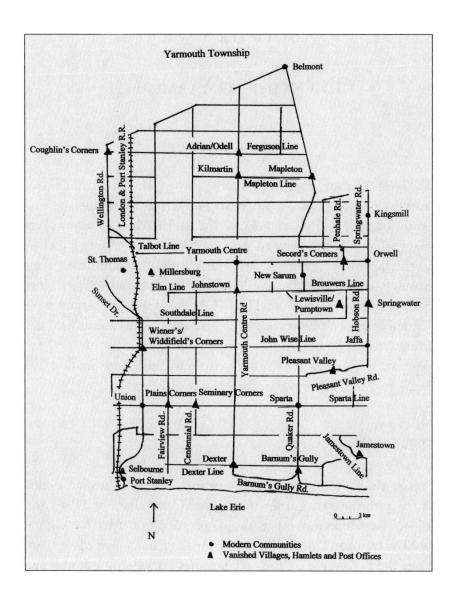

Yarmouth Township

Belmont

Coughlin's Corners

Wellington Rd.

London & Port Stanley R.R.

Adrian/Odell   Ferguson Line

Kilmartin   Mapleton

Mapleton Line

Penhale Rd.

Springwater Rd.

Kingsmill

Talbot Line   Yarmouth Centre   Secord's Corners   Orwell

St. Thomas

Millersburg

New Sarum

Sunset Dr.

Elm Line   Johnstown

Brouwers Line

Lewisville/
Pumptown

Hobson Rd

Springwater

Southdale Line

Yarmouth Centre Rd

Wiener's/
Widdifield's Corners

John Wise Line   Jaffa

Pleasant Valley

Union   Plains Corners   Seminary Corners   Sparta

Pleasant Valley Rd.

Sparta Line

Fairview Rd.

Centennial Rd.

Quaker Rd.

Jamestown Line

Jamestown

Dexter   Barnum's Gully

Selbourne   Dexter Line

Port Stanley

Barnum's Gully Rd.

Lake Erie

0   3 km

N

• Modern Communities
▲ Vanished Villages, Hamlets and Post Offices

136

Barnum's Gully

The hamlet of Barnum's Gully sat at the corner of Quaker Road and Barnum Gully Line. Its best-known feature was its spectacular natural setting on the shore of Lake Erie.

William Barnum and his wife, Phoebe Dowling, came from New York state in 1825 and settled on the west side of Quaker Road south of Dexter Line. They raised a large family. Before they died, they left a large portion of land to their eldest son, Eliphalet. He and his wife, Amelia, continued to live at the homestead not far from the lake. Eliphalet is said to have been a "colourful" character. Tall and lanky, with long arms, he could "out-cradle" any man, referring to the action involved in cutting hay or grain with a scythe. It is claimed that during harvest he made five dollars a day at a time when most farm help only earned that much a month. One day, a neighbour named James Dangerfield decided to borrow that same amount from Eliphalet, who was not at home at the time. Amelia found the sum of money for Dangerfield and gave it to him without asking for a receipt. When her husband returned, he was enraged because of her oversight, and began hounding his neighbour for either a receipt or repayment. The ill feeling between the two men was the talk of the neighbourhood for years.[2]

A log school was built in 1840 on land north of the Barnum homestead and close to Sparta. After a few years, however, a new structure was erected on the east side of Quaker Road, south of Dexter Line and the first teacher to be hired was Alice Bisell. The property on which the school was built originally belonged to a Mr. Sagar, who had been one of Butler's Rangers[3] during the War of 1812.[4] He lived there until he died and was buried on his land. When the school was being consructed, his remains were exhumed and reinterred at Sparta Cemetery. Eventually a third school went up across a ravine, near the second one. It officially became SS No. 4 Yarmouth but was called Barnum's Gully School in later years.

Both Methodists and Freewill Baptists used the local school for services. In 1883, an Anglican church was established on the west side of the road south of Dexter Line, and later a Methodist congregation built on the east side of the road. At its height,

Barnum's Gully was named after William Barnum, who emigrated to the area from New York in 1825.

Barnum's Corners, as it was then called, consisted of a school, two churches, several homes, and a general store.

The gully was formed accidentally when a small ditch was dug to drain what was considered to be an excessively wet field on William Barnum's farm. The wet area disappeared, but so did much of the land. Acres washed away, and eventually the lakeshore road had to be moved farther inland. The gully became a deep gorge enclosing a small stream that flows into Lake Erie. It is about a mile long, and the land along its edge is still very prone to erosion. At one time the road continued across the stream, but continued erosion destroyed the roadbed, and now it runs around the north end of the gully. During the 1860s, soldiers stationed at Port Stanley and Port Bruce patrolled this road to stop expected Fenian raids.[5]

Barnum's Gully was probably too close to Sparta and Port Bruce to amount to any great size. Eventually, the Anglican church became a temperance hall in Union, and the Methodist church was moved to Jaffa, where it later became a home. Barnum's Gully School closed in 1968, and young people started studying in Sparta. The building became a residence but has since been removed. Barnum Gully Woods is still a small woodlot along the Lake Erie shore known for its spectacular ground cover of ferns.

Coughlin's or Townline Corners
See Southwold Township.

Dexter

The location of Dexter will be familiar to many travellers driving along the road between Port Stanley and Port Bruce. There is still a road sign to announce what was once a sizeable community at Concession 2 Yarmouth (now Dexter Line) and Centre Side Line (now Yarmouth Centre Road).

Records contain an unusual story explaining the name. It is said to honour the city of Exeter in Devon, England, birthplace of settlers James and Sarah Jones, and is supposed to be a combination of the French prefix *d'* ("from" or "of'") and Exeter.[6]

The Joneses emigrated from England in 1850 and settled on the northwest corner of the Dexter intersection. When Sarah first saw her pioneer farm in the wilderness, she was depressed. "Many a good cry I had. It was so lonely and so different from what I had been accustomed to, but I got used to it, and gradually the comforts and conveniences came to us."[7] A story illustrates her early hardships. Eggs sold for 5¢ a dozen and butter for 8¢ a pound. Receiving cash for produce, however, was an almost unheard of occurrence in those days. One time, however, the local storekeeper did Sarah a favour and gave her cash for twenty dozen of her eggs at 5¢ per dozen; she needed the money to pay for shoes for one of her many children.[8] After James died in 1892, Sarah continued to run the farm with her son Henry. She died in 1918 at the age of ninety-four, having lived to see Dexter grow into a village and then decline.

A post office named Dexter opened at the intersection on August 1, 1858, under William Teetzel. Later postmasters were William Collier, Nelson Parker, Lewis Jones, Lindley C. Lanning, Isaac H. Jones, and C.D. Parker. Mail was tri-weekly. By 1865 there was a small business section listed in *Fuller's Counties of Elgin and Norfolk Directory*: Dexter entries were Frank Barrett, broom manufacturer; Wellington Parker, blacksmith; John Pfeffer, cooper; Hugh Stephens, blacksmith; and William Spatler, hotelkeeper. The village had seventy-five residents.[9] By 1872, there was a general store at Dexter, and eventually there were two general stores and two blacksmiths. The cooperage was on the northeast corner; one blacksmith was on the southeast corner, with the other one on the southwest corner, east of the site of the current hall. In 1845, a frame school, officially SS No. 3, was built on land donated by the Parker family. It was replaced by a brick structure in 1877 and became known as Dexter School.

A Baptist church was built when Lyman Lewis donated half the funds for its construction in 1865. For the next twenty-five years, the Baptist congregation would hold services there, the land having been contributed by Benjamin Fisher. When the edifice was completed, it was discovered that $500 was lacking to pay outstanding bills. The man in charge of the building fund, Mr. Barrett, went to Lewis's homestead on Lakeshore Road, only to find him standing sadly beside the remains of a valuable mare that had died. Feeling badly about troubling him, Barrett said, "I hate to tell you my errand." But the generous Lewis, using the body of the dead horse for a desk, wrote a note for another $100.[10] The Baptist minister boarded at Lewis's home for free and had use of a horse and buggy.

A Methodist congregation built this church (now Dexter United) in the late 1880s.

In 1875, Methodist settlers decided they too wanted their own place of worship. William Armstrong donated land for the church site and Providence Church was built to the west of the intersection. In time, the Baptist congregation dwindled considerably, and Presbyterians and Anglicans began holding services at that church and did so until about 1892. At that time, the Presbyterian minister, a Mr. Bloodsworth, decided to discontinue services, so the Methodists, Presbyterians, Anglicans, and Baptists joined together to form Dexter Methodist Church. The edifice was modernized in 1920 — the structure was raised, a basement installed, and the outside covered in brick and stucco.

Dexter Community Hall, a centre for the community, still stands.

Like other small villages, Dexter did not survive the rise of the automobile, and businesses gradually closed. In 1902, the general store burned,[11] and the post office closed on April 30, 1918. Today, Dexter United is providing services on the northwest corner. The 1877 school is still standing on the south side of the road, west of the intersection; it is now a private residence. A hall — the community centre — remains on the southwest corner, to the east of the school, along with a few houses.

Jamestown

Jamestown is one of Elgin County's best-known vanished villages. It is on Jamestown Line, set in a deep valley three miles upriver from Port Bruce, along the banks of Catfish Creek.

It was James Chrysler, who was born an American but later became a wealthy merchant in St. Thomas, who chose this location for a village in 1835. He spotted the creek's potential to supply water-power for mills, and there was plenty of timber available locally. But first he built a distillery, as there was great demand for whisky in early Upper Canada. Soon the Jamestown whisky was known throughout the province, selling for 25¢ a gallon.[12] The distillery also helped support local farmers by providing a nearby market for their grain.

Chrysler constructed a dam across Catfish Creek, then built a sawmill on one side of the stream and a gristmill on the other. He next set up warehouses and wharves along the bank of the creek. Local farmers now had an active marketplace for their corn, wheat, and timber. Soon Chrysler established a general store as well. He had engaged surveyor Daniel Hanvey to divide the site into lots in 1835. As Chrysler's businesses required many labourers, these lots were quickly taken up by the workers. Soon Jamestown was created and named after its founder. *Smith's Canadian Gazetteer* for 1846 describes it as "a small settlement near the south-east corner of the township of Yarmouth, on Catfish Creek, about one mile from Lake Erie, contains a grist and saw mill, distiller, and about ten houses." There were only three other communities in Yarmouth Township — St. Thomas, Port Stanley, and Sparta.[13]

Soon other businessmen were attracted to the area. John Oille set up a blacksmith and wagon-making shop, and there is also said to have been a hotel.[14] Scows, built in Jamestown by Henry Carter, plied up and down Catfish Creek, carrying cargoes of flour, lumber, and whisky to Port Bruce, where the goods were transferred to lake vessels and shipped to Buffalo. A post office was opened on September 6, 1852, with William Jones as postmaster. Jamestown was at its peak.

Other than Chrysler himself, the village's best-known resident was Charles Freeman, a boxer — the "Canadian Giant" — who had worked in Chrysler's sawmill as a teenager. Being 6'10" tall and weighing 325 pounds, he was spectacularly strong; he reputedly could throw a horse a distance of ten feet.[15] He is probably the Charles Freeman who became a boxer and fought William Perry, "the Tipton Slasher," on December 6, 1842, in Bishop's Stortford, England; the press described the contest as the world's first heavyweight championship under London Prize Ring rules. "Freeman lifted him [Perry] off the ground as if he had been a child." The two men were in the ring later that year, and Freeman won this time too. He never boxed again, saying he "he did not care for the role of bruiser."[16] He went on to become a stage actor and circus performer[17] and in 1844 died of tuberculosis.[18]

Eventually, Jamestown's profits started to diminish. Port Bruce was flourishing, and Jamestown could no longer compete for the shipping business. Although Jamestown was on the Catfish, it was not on a main road. As well, timber for the sawmill was scarce, as the forests were being depleted. The tax on whisky increased[19] and repairing the dam and mill was a very expensive venture.

Chrysler sold his property to James Cotton of Port Stanley, but it changed hands frequently afterwards. The distillery also had many owners over the years, later operators being Sylvester Rykert and James Durdle ("Whisky Jim").[20] The business finally went bankrupt when one of the partners disappeared with the funds.[21] Lyman Young took over both the gristmill and the sawmill but discovered there was little need for the latter, as much of the local timber had already been harvested. As an alternative, he converted the mill to one in which flax was prepared for linen and papermaking. However, the dam itself was costly to maintain, repairs being required frequently because of damage caused by running water. In 1864, Young is the only businessman mentioned under Jamestown on Tremaine's *Map of the County of Elgin*.[22] Thomas Pineo bought the entire former Chrysler property for $2,400 in 1864.[23] He tore down the mills and smaller buildings but left the distillery to run down. He and his wife converted the old hotel into a home, where they lived until he died in 1892.

In 1877, the *Illustrated Historical Atlas* reported, "Jamestown, a flourishing little place in 1840, has gone down to decay."[24] And

The bridge over Catfish Creek at Jamestown.

by 1895, the site had become a farm, although there were still "a few decayed timbers on the banks of the Catfish, and the name, Jamestown ... still clings to the neighbouring hills."[25]

A serious accident took place in the autumn of 1892 in the Jamestown Valley; late one evening William Ashton was crossing the old wooden bridge over the Catfish with his threshing machine. Suddenly the beams, which were very rotten, gave way, and Ashton, along with his horses and thresher, fell twenty feet into the stream below. One horse was killed, and much of the machine fell on top of poor Ashton, injuring him so badly that his life was seriously threatened. However, he did recover, albeit very slowly. A new wooden span was built at a cost of $1,640.[26]

The steep Jamestown hill on the east side of the bridge provided many adventures for early automobile drivers. Apparently, it was easier to climb while driving in reverse, and historian Hugh Sims records that in 1925 his father backed up the hill in his Model T Ford.[27]

Today, the Jamestown Line meandering through Jamestown Valley is one of the more scenic drives in Elgin County. The number of "No Trespassing" signs in the area suggests the local people have had troubles with passersby stopping to look for traces of Jamestown.

The challenging Jamestown hill; some early automobile drivers found it easier to climb in reverse.

Johnstown

Johnstown stood on Elm Line between Centre Side Line (now Yarmouth Centre Road) and Quaker Road. It consisted of a sawmill, cheese factory, and schoolhouse.

The name is said to have come from the large number of men named John in the area. John Marlatt, his son John, Jr., John McVey, John Taylor, John C. Caughill, and John Hess lived there in the nineteenth century.

Tragedy occurred on November 6, 1878, when young Margaret McVey set out to bring in the cows. When night came and the cows were nowhere to be seen, her father became anxious and went looking for her. He and the neighbours explored frantically all night. The county constable, Freeman Taylor, organized a search of the countryside that lasted for days, but no trace was ever found of the girl — only a milk pail at the edge of some nearby woods. [28]

Little is known of the cheese factory or sawmill, only that they did exist at an earlier time. The Johnstown School, SS No. 12, was built of white bricks in 1907, on the east side of Yarmouth Centre

Seth Lewis built a sawmill, cooperage, pump factory, and shingle mill on his farm. As well, in 1891 he and his wife, Priscilla, had a brick house constructed for themselves, a sign of their growing prosperity. Joel built a sawmill, woodworking mill, cider and vinegar works, machine shop, blacksmith shop, wagon-maker's shop, and brickyard. He too had a large home erected on his property for himself and his wife Hannah; the bricks were made at his own brickyard. Joel was very generous, and many people stayed for free overnight in one of the many spare bedrooms on the second floor of his large, Georgian-style house. He also liked to trade, and people from miles around would come to deal with him. In this way, he acquired a large pair of boots that had belonged to Charles Freeman, the local giant who once worked at Chrysler's sawmill (see Jamestown).[29]

Page's 1877 *Illustrated Historical Atlas* shows a road going west from Hobson Road, at the end of which is a sawmill, and it indicates the brickyard just to the north of this location.[30] Joel operated this farm and his businesses until his death in 1886. Though no longer hubs of industrial activity, both Seth and Joel's houses are still standing on the west side of Hobson Road, north of Southdale Line.

Mapleton
See South Dorchester Township.

Millersburg

Elgin County's largest community, the county town of St. Thomas, first developed around what is now St. Thomas' Church on Walnut Street and spread from there. St. Thomas became a village in 1852, and a town in 1861. It has certainly grown over the years, having reached a population of 36,000, but has never annexed as many surrounding communities as did London in Middlesex County. Only once did St. Thomas swallow up a potential rival.

What is today the east end of St. Thomas was sparsely settled in the mid-nineteenth century, largely open countryside miles from town. The first settlers were members of the Miller family, who

Millersburg is shown east of St. Thomas in 1864 on Tremaine's Map of the County of Elgin. *John B. Miller's land is to the north of the word "Millersburg." St. Thomas annexed its rival in 1871.*

acquired much of that land. Edward Miller's original house stood just off present-day Alma Street; John Miller's red-brick farmhouse was also nearby. There were very few businesses in the area although Luke Bishop had a market garden on what is now Kains Street. Another early enterprise was Mihell's Tailor Shop. The area was known as Millersburg by at least 1864, as evidenced by Tremaine's *Map of the County of Elgin* of that year.

Then, in the late 1860s, the Canada Southern Railway announced plans to link Detroit and Niagara Falls with a line going right through St. Thomas. The railway purchased a large block of land for its station and car shops. The area to the north of these buildings then began to be developed in earnest. The Miller farm was surveyed and laid out in lots. Labourers, artisans, and mechanics came and built houses for themselves and their families near the tracks. The railway itself encouraged workers to come from eastern Canada, the United States, Britain, and Ireland. In 1870, the combined population of St. Thomas and Millersburg was 2,000.[31] But in no time at all, the former agricultural area was growing faster than old St. Thomas, and the new village had 10,000 residents.[32]

The dividing line between the two communities Millersburg and St. Thomas is not easy to define. It has been given variously as St. Catherine Street, the London & Port Stanley Railway tracks, and Manitoba Street. Whatever the boundary, businessmen in St. Thomas started to notice that people and trade were choosing Millersburg over their community. Merchants such as William Coyne, a Liberal, and John Midgeley, a Tory, debated one another in front of their shops when business was slack; what to do about the situation? St. Thomas drygoods merchants such as Pollock and Baird, James Carrie, and J. and W. Mickleborough were also concerned about the locations of their stores.[33] Would Millersburgers go two miles to shop? Or would they start up their own enterprises? East-enders themselves had already complained about having to travel all the way to William Street to go to a market. The market controversy went on for years, with possible sites being rejected by both sides as being too far to the other end. At one meeting a prominent west-ender referred to the newcomers as "east-end paupers," a remark that nearly caused a riot; east-enders retaliated by referring to westenders as "back-numbers," "aristocrats," and "blue beards."[34] East-enders had also made it clear they were not going to church in St. Thomas — it was too far away. The railway had assisted them by allowing the station to be used for religious services until regular churches could be built in the neighbourhood.[35]

Eventually, the two communities started to meet in the middle, and the centre of town moved eastward. It became obvious that the village would soon be annexed by the town. What concerned Millersburgers was that they had little debt while St. Thomas had considerable. Accordingly, at the time of annexation in March 1871, St. Thomas agreed that Millersburg would not be taxed for the debts of old St. Thomas,[36] thus different tax rates coexisted. Millersburg became known as St. David's Ward, and on March 4, 1881, St. Thomas became a city.

Today, the former Millersburg is not distinguishable from the rest of St. Thomas. The only reminder is the tiny Miller Street between Nolan and Redan streets. St. Thomas's old railway station has become the Elgin County Railroad Museum.

Plains Corners

The intersection of Sparta Line and Fairview Road consisted of a Baptist church and sawmill. The church has been on the southwest corner in various buildings since 1831 and still exists today. In the nineteenth century, the sawmill was just north of the corners on the west side of the road and was operated by the Zavitz and Hawkins families.

There has been a Plains Baptist Church at Plains Corners since 1831.

Pleasant Valley

This early pioneer settlement was on Concession 5 Yarmouth (now Pleasant Valley Road) between Springwater and Quaker roads. It was known for its mills on Catfish Creek.

The land in the area was granted to Colonel James Baby (pronounced "Bawbee") for his service to the British during the American Revolution. Mills were built there in the early nineteenth century, but there seems to be a little confusion about who constructed and owned them. A gristmill may have been erected for Baby by Cornelius Mills and may have been operated by a Mr. S. Brown, whose first name is sometimes spelled Sebisky, Selbenky, and Selberky.[37] Alternatively, either Brown or Mills may have built a gristmill himself. The facility was much appreciated by early settlers, who otherwise had to go to Long Point by boat to have their grain ground into flour. The structure was on the south side of the road at the foot of the east hill, and the mill pond stretched north up the valley on the east side. Later a sawmill also drew waterpower from this pond.

As the settlement expanded, a side street was laid out, and three houses were erected for mill hands. David Adams took over the property and is said to have established a post office and general store[38] there, although there is no official record of a post office called Pleasant Valley.

As in many milling communities, future development was prevented by an eventual scarcity of timber, which in turn led to the end of the sawmill. Without ongoing maintenance, the mill dam weakened and was eventually destroyed, probably in a flood. The buildings gradually fell into decay and disappeared.

This area today is still called Pleasant Valley, as in Pleasant Valley Road and Pleasant Valley Trout and Pheasant Farm.

Secord's Corners

The intersection of Talbot Line and Penhale Road was named after the pioneer Secord family and was the location of a school and brickyard. The school was to the east on the south side of the road and was also used for Baptist services. The nearby brickyard was established by William Skates, but over time it had many owners.

Selbourne

The village of Selbourne was north of Port Stanley and is now part of it, but in the first half of the nineteenth century it was larger that the port. The community occupied land on both sides of Kettle Creek north of where Warren Street is today.

The origin of the name is not entirely certain. It has been stated over the years that it was named after Lord Selbourne, but that title did not come into existence until 1872.[39] It is likely the moniker comes from a town in east Hampshire, England,[40] but whether an early settler hailed from there is not known. The name is sometimes spelled Selborne, like the English village.

James Hamilton and John Warren built the first mill on the east side of the creek about 1817. For a while, the fledgling community was Talbot Mills, after Hamilton and Warren's business. Milling was always an important industry at Selbourne. The best known facility, a mill, which also survived the longest, went up on the west side of the valley

Courtesy of Elgin County Archives C3Sb6B1F18.

The Harding Mill at Selbourne, early 1900s, now moved and renovated into a home.

on the way to Fingal about 1831. Originally, it was to be a gristmill, but it was taken over by a Mr. Earnshaw, who turned it into a woollen mill and made blankets. Later it was purchased by Thomas Harding. By 1857, it was the Phoenix Flour Mill. It changed hands many times before being bought by George Bell in 1925. The mill pond was always a popular place to swim in summer and skate in winter.

Kettle Creek must have been wider and deeper then than it is today. One of the first industries at Selbourne was shipbuilding, so the waterway had to have been navigable by fairly large ships. Hamilton and Warren (see Tyrconnell) operated a shipyard at Selbourne where they built the 90-ton schooner *Stirling* and launched it in 1827.

The first land purchase in the area was made by Joseph Smith. He bought 2,200 acres from Colonel Mahlon Burwell in 1822. He first disposed of land to David Anderson, who by 1833 had a tavern on his property, on the west side of the creek at Selbourne. The first store at Selbourne was built by John Wintermute, Smith's son-in-law. The foundry, established by a Mr. Hornby, was also later

An advertisement for James Turville's store at Selbourne. Evangelical Pioneer, *January 7, 1848.*

JAMES TURVILL, Selborne, near Port Stan-
ley, keeps constantly on hand a good assortment of
DRY GOODS, GROCERIES, HARDWARE,
And every other article usually kept in country stores; all
of which will be sold *Cheap as the Cheapest,* for Cash.
Agent for the sale of the
GENUINE MOFFATT'S, BRANDRETH'S, & LEE'S PILLS,
And most other kinds of Patent Medicines.
A good assortment of LUMBER always on hand.
A superior CARDING MACHINE (made by M'Lauchlan
& Co. Ancaster), *nearly new,* will be sold cheap.
Also for sale, 100 acres of LAND, west half of Lot No.
23, north of Egremont Road, being the graded road from
London to Port Sarnia.
Also for sale, a HOUSE and LOT in St. Thomas, on the
principal street, being corner of King and Talbot streets, oc-
cupied at present as a Tailor's shop.
Also for sale, that well-known Grist and Flouring MILL,
on Third Concession, Malahide, belonging to Wm. Turvill.
*All those whose Notes and Accounts are past due will
please pay, or else ——*
JAMES TURVILL.
Selborne, Jan. 7, 1848.   2

operated by John Wintermute, who turned out many ships' anchors and other marine fittings. A dry goods store was constructed by James Turville. There were shoemakers named Abernathy and Cribb, two blacksmiths, a wagon maker, a tailor, and two doctors. A Mr. N. Hussie kept a drugstore and one of two local distilleries; the other was operated by William Smith, son of Joseph.

One of these distilleries was referred to as "Still Hill." It became a gathering place for local men, and according to one story an elderly fellow became somewhat of an annoyance. He had lost his job, no longer had money for drinks, and had used all his credit. He found a way, however, to obtain his refreshments for free. Whisky was sold in a small wooden keg for a dollar. The man took his keg and changed it so it had two compartments, one of which he filled with water; then he went to the distillery and filled his keg with whisky. When he was leaving, the proprietor challenged him and told him to pay for it. When the old man replied that he had no money, he was told to pour his keg back into the vat. This he did with loud cursing and berating of the staff. Then he went on his way with half a keg of whisky under his arm, leaving the distillery richer by half a keg of water.[41]

Colonel John Bostwick founded the community that became Port Stanley. He was a surveyor, sheriff, militia officer, and an associate of Colonel Talbot and Mahlon Burwell. He was granted two lots on the east side of Kettle Creek in 1804 but did not settle there until 1812. His was the first house at Port Stanley, built in 1817 on what is now Main Street. He eventually laid out a town site and offered lots for sale. In time, the name Port Stanley was chosen to honour Lord Stanley, a friend of Colonel Talbot. Stanley is said to have visited the port.[42]

Initially, however, settlers were more attracted to Selbourne. There seem to have been three main reasons for this. First, Bostwick was charging a very high price for his land at the mouth of Kettle Creek, and land upstream at Selbourne was cheaper. Second, Selbourne had more flat, agricultural land, better to build and farm on, whereas the port area was marshy and hilly. Third, there was better opportunity to build mills on the creek than at the port, and mills were very important pioneer industries. As well, Selbourne was a mile closer to the Talbot Trail, the main road between Port Talbot and York (now Toronto).

By 1846, Selbourne was at its peak. *Smith's Canadian Gazetteer* for that year describes "Selborne or Talbot Mills" as a "village in the townships of Yarmouth and Southwold, situated on Kettle Creek, close to the plank road — one mile and half from Port Stanley." It lists a gristmill, two distilleries, a foundry, two doctors, one druggist, two stores, two taverns, two blacksmiths, one wagon maker, one shoemaker, and one tailor.[43] Port Stanley, however, was already much larger; its usefulness as a harbour had at last been recognized.

When the London & Port Stanley Railway was built to Port Stanley, it did not actually run all the way there but terminated at Selbourne. The tracks could not be extended to the harbour until Kettle Creek was bridged and various rights of way had been sorted out, and a bridge had to be constructed across the creek midway between the harbour and Selbourne. Meanwhile the railway had permission to have its freight cars hauled by horses along the road from Selbourne to the harbour. There was a tollgate on this road, and the price to pass through was 7¢ per wagon.[44]

Disasters brought about Selbourne's decline. In 1850, a flood changed the course of Kettle Creek and wrought considerable destruction. Much business activity declined after this. A fire in 1854 consumed most of the village, and a serious flood in 1855 destroyed what was left. That same year, huge chunks of ice came down and caused much additional damage. One of these floods destroyed Hamilton and Warren's old mill. However, the mill at the extreme western edge of the village survived, as that area had a higher elevation.

By the time the devastation was over, the London & Port Stanley had finally been built right through to the lake. The direct access to the harbour discouraged the rebuilding of Selbourne, and the community was doomed. Afterwards the area was generally known as "Suckertown," presumably because of the suckers, a freshwater fish related to the carp in Kettle Creek[45] — but perhaps also a pejorative term for its residents?

Selbourne Park in northern Port Stanley is one of the few reminders of the village that once rivalled the port community in size and business.

The area has been taken over by Port Stanley. There are a few reminders of the former village. One is the Selbourne ball diamond on the south side of Warren Street. Another is Selbourne Street to the east of and parallel to Main Street. Another reminder, though greatly changed, is the old Harding Mill. After George Bell died in 1942, the mill stood empty for a while. It was the Smith family that dismantled it and moved it to a location on Orchard Beach overlooking the lake. The intention was to use it as a summer home, but severe erosion threatened this site, and the mill was moved to its present location, 181 Brayside Street, in 1957.

Springwater (see Malahide Township)

Wiener's or Widdifield's Corners

 Wiener's Corners was at the intersection of Concession 5 Yarmouth (later County Road 45, now John Wise Line) and the Port Stanley and London Gravel Road (later Highway 4, now Sunset Road).

 The Widdifield family bought the land on the southeast corner of the intersection in 1824. John Widdifield[46] realized in 1859 that there was a "dry" spot between the communities of St. Thomas and Union and set about rectifying the situation. He built a large two-storey brick hotel on the southeast corner — Widdifield House. The inn had a two-storey verandah across the entire front that faced the Gravel Road and two semi-circular windows in the gable ends. A hand pump was nearby for the convenience of watering horses.

 Widdifield's home was south of the inn. It was of unusual construction, being faced with quarried stone on the west side only while the rest was ordinary fieldstone. It is said that when the courthouse had been under construction in St. Thomas, the quarried

The Wiener family home at Wiener's Corners.

stone used for it was brought up the lake by ship to Port Stanley, and from there was hauled by teamsters to the site. Somehow on the way a few stones were left every once in a while at Widdifield's Corners in exchange for "something that would cure a dry throat"[47] — but not enough stones to finish all four sides of the house.

In 1870, Widdifield sold his inn and land to Charles Wiener, and the inn became Wiener's Halfway House, which the new owner and his sons Charles, Jr., and Frank operated for forty-eight years. This establishment became the headquarters of the St. Thomas Gun Club, and pigeon shoots were held on the property. It was also a meeting place for a local bicycle club whose members, after peddling miles over dusty township roads, required a rest stop.[48]

A blacksmith shop was operated by a Mr. Jones on the lot south of the stone house. According to one story, Francis George Jones bought an acre of land in 1849 and another half acre in 1858 and ran his smithy and wagon factory on this site with the help of William Mandeville.[49] Another version states the blacksmith was John Jones and that the lot wasn't purchased until the 1870s.[50] A general store was positioned on the southwest corner of the intersection. A school, probably SS No. 17, is shown in the 1877 *Illustrated Historical Atlas* to be north of the intersection on the east side of the road. A Mr. and Mrs. Sebastian Egner lived in a cottage near the corner of the Wiener farm. Egner was a shoemaker; his wife was a sister of Mrs. Charles Wiener, Sr.

The London & Port Stanley Railway tracks ran just to the west of the intersection starting in 1855, and a station was built near Concession 5, but Norman Station was not an important stop and thus did not encourage expansion of the hamlet.

The inn burned down in 1918 and was never rebuilt. Today, this area is a suburb of St. Thomas. It is likely there are more people living there now than there ever were in the nineteenth century. The Wiener home, still standing on the east side of the road south of the intersection, is one of the few older buildings around the intersection and is still owned by the family.

NOTES

Introduction

1.   *Elgin County: An Introduction. Research Report No. 1* (Elgin County Local Government Study, 1975).

2.   *Township of Yarmouth Centennial* (Yarmouth Township, 1967).

3.   Alan Rayburn, *Place Names of Ontario* (Toronto: University of Toronto Press, 1997), 108.

Chapter One: Township of Aldborough

1.   Kenneth Cameron, *English Place Names* (London: B.T. Batsford, 1977), 112.

2.   Rayburn, *Place Names*, 7.

3.   "United Church of Canada: Elgin Presbytery," a photocopy of a typescript at London Room, Central Public Library, London, Ontario.

4.   The Canada Company, a land settlement firm based in England, began operations in 1826. John Galt, the novelist, adventurer, and lobbyist from Scotland, was sent to Upper Canada (now Ontario) as its first commissioner. The Canada Company was responsible for settling over two million acres of land in Upper Canada. One of its legacies was the founding of towns in the area, such as Guelph, Goderich, and Stratford. For more information, see Robert C. Lee,

The Canada Company and the Huron Tract, 1826–1853: Personalities, Profits and Politics (Toronto: Natural Heritage Books, 2004).

5. Harley Lashbrook, *Aldborough: The Township with a Past* (West Lorne, ON: Webco Publications, 2001), 89.

6. Wilfred C. Johnston, *Catholic Churches of West Elgin* (London, ON: Diocese of London, 1979), n.p.

7. Ibid.

8. H. Lashbrook, *Aldborough*, 79.

9. Johnston, *Catholic Churches of West Elgin*.

10. Ibid.

11. H. Lashbrook, *Aldborough*, 94.

12. Ibid, 91.

13. Crinan Women's Institute, Tweedsmuir History, vol. I, 111. www.elgin.ca/tweedsmuir/aldborough.html, accessed December 12, 2007.

14. J.H. MacIntyre (ed.), *The Pioneer Days in Aldborough* (Aldborough Old Boys Association, 1933) 74. Another story states that the Crinan post office was first located in a building owned by a Mr. Paups, who possessed a grocery store that failed. Keith Kelly and Irving Thomas, *A Postal History of West Elgin* (West Elgin Historical and Genealogical Society, 1999), 8.

15. Crinan Women's Institute, Tweedsmuir History, vol. I, 136. The source states that Woodgreen was in Ekfrid Township, but it was actually in Mosa. See Jennifer Grainger, *Vanished Villages of Middlesex* (Toronto: Natural Heritage Books, 2002) 200. Woodgreen was not officially named until 1894.

16. H. Lashbrook, *Aldborough*, 132.

17. Crinan Women's Institute, Tweedsmuir History, 51.

18. His name also appears as Mr. Hoddish.

19.   MacIntyre, *Pioneer Days*, 74.

20.   Personal communication with Catherine McMillan, November 13, 2007.

21.   John Kenneth Galbraith, *The Scotch* (Toronto: Macmillan of Canada, 1964), 11.

22.   Tena McKillop, "School History," *West Lorne Sun*, June 19, 1967.

23.   The Canada Southern Railway was a 229-mile-long system connecting Amherstburg on the Detroit River to Fort Erie, with another sixty-three miles connecting Courtright to St. Thomas. Built mainly through the efforts of promoter William Thompson in 1871–72, it passed through every Elgin township except Bayham. When the first Canada Southern locomotive ran through St. Thomas in August 1872, it catapulted a small community into a railway boom town. The railway brought prosperity to all the communities along its line. Unfortunately, it never prospered because of the recession of the 1870s, and was taken over by the Michigan Central Railroad in 1882. For more information, see Wayne Paddon, *Glimpses into St. Thomas Railway History: The Canada Southern Railway*, vol. I (Paddon Books, 1989) and, also by the same author, *"Steam and Petticoats" 1840–1890: The Early Railway Era in Southwestern Ontario* (Paddon Books, 1977).

24.   A cord is a unit of wood equal to a stack 4 feet by 4 feet by 8 feet, or 128 cubic feet.

25.   MacIntyre, *Pioneer Days*, 44.

26.   Floreen Carter, *Place Names of Ontario* (London, ON: Phelps Publishing, 1985), 107.

27.   Paul Baldwin, "Cycle Historic Elgin: With Local History Essays and Suggested Routes," self-published pamphlet, n.d., 11.

28.   Nancy Lashbrook, *West Lorne: 90 Years a Village* (West Lorne, ON: Webco Publications, 1997) 5. His gravestone at Churchville spells Bismarck without the "c" — Bismark. The name of the village was sometimes rendered this way as well.

29.   West Lorne Women's Institute, Tweedsmuir History, vol. I, a

photocopy of a typescript at the London Room, Central Public Library, London.

30.   John Field, *Place Names of Great Britain and Ireland* (Newton Abbott, England: David and Charles, 1980), 108.

31.   Harley Lashbrook, personal communication, September 6, 2007.

32.   Hugh J. Sims, *Sims' History of Elgin County* (St. Thomas, ON: Elgin County Library, 1984) vol. III, 201. Note that maps such as *Scarborough's Survey of Middlesex and Elgin Counties* in 1910 continued to use out-of-date information and refer to Bismarck Station after the name changed.

33.   Part of the railway empire established by Cornelius Vanderbilt, the Michigan Central took over the Canada Southern in 1882. The rails were later leased by the New York Central and officially made part of that line in 1930. For more information, see Paddon, *Glimpses*, and Douglas N.W. Smith, *The New York Central in Canada: Southern Ontario Lines*, vol. I (Ottawa: Trackside Canada, 1998).

34.   American distiller Hiram Walker created the Lake Erie and Detroit River Railway (LEDR) in 1885; it was to run from St. Thomas to Windsor. The railway was intended to transport raw materials from Ontario farmlands to the distillery as well as to carry cattle and lumber for export to American markets. The rail line had reached St. Thomas by 1895. In 1903 the LEDR, or "Booze Line," was taken over by the Pere Marquette, a railroad organized in Michigan. In 1904, the Pere Marquette secured running rights over the Michigan Central line as well. The Chesapeake and Ohio Railroad took over the Pere Marquette in 1947. See E.B. George, *Vignettes of the Old Pere Marquette in Canada* (London, ON: F.J. Ram, 1990), and Ron Brown, *Ghost Railways of Ontario* (Toronto: Polar Bear Press, 1998).

35.   H. Lashbrook, *Aldborough*, 273.

36.   Several smaller American railways consolidated to form the New York Central in 1853. It took over the Michigan Central Railroad, which it had been leasing for many years, in 1930. See Smith, *New York Central*.

37.   H. Lashbrook, *Aldborough*, 274.

Chapter Two: Township of Bayham

1. G.H. Armstrong, *The Origin and Meaning of Place Names in Canada* (Toronto: Macmillan, 1930) 25. Note that Camden West Township in Kent County and Camden East Township in Lennox and Addington County were also named after this man; Rayburn, *Place Names*, 53.

2. Giles A. Hume, *A Capsule History of East Elgin* (St. Thomas, ON: Elgin County Library Board, 1975), 8.

3. For more information on the significance of oak trees in the building of wooden boats and on the construction of early lake vessels, see Don Bamford, *Freshwater Heritage: A History of Sail on the Great Lakes, 1670–1918* (Toronto: Natural Heritage Books/The Dundurn Group, 2007) chapter 15, 131–60.

4. Kirk Barons, "Pioneer Churches and a Brief History of Bayham Township" (1977) 25, a pamphlet in the London Room, Central Public Library, London.

5. Ibid.

6. Ibid.

7. Corinth Women's Institute, Tweedsmuir History, 47.

8. Firby Cemetery, Bayham Township, Elgin County, Ontario. See www.elginogs.ca/cemeteries/bayham/firby.htm, accessed June 25, 2007.

9. "Hamlets Villages and Towns." www.elginconnects.ca/portal/entry. php?w=EdisonMuseumHamletsVillagesandTowns&e_id=240, accessed December 15, 2007. However, according to Corinth Women's Institute, Tweedsmuir History, 29, the factory closed about 1930.

10. The Plank Road opened in 1851 between Ingersoll and Port Burwell. It was constructed of planks from the sawmill of E.D. Tillson of Tillsonburg. It was an improvement over the earlier corduroy road, but the planks were still so noisy that local residents could *hear* a stagecoach approaching long before they could see it. See Sims, *History*, vol. II, 90.

11. The New Connexionists were a branch of Methodism founded by William Thom and Alexander Kilham in 1797 in northern England. Formerly Wesleyan Methodists, Thom and Kilham objected to perceived Wesleyan subservience to the Church of England; they also thought decisions such as the receiving and expelling of members and the election of officers should be permitted on a local level. In 1851, New Connexion adherents in Canada West (formerly Upper Canada) numbered 8,600, and, in 1861, the figure had risen to 25,000. See Neil Semple, *The Lord's Dominion: The History of Canadian Methodism* (Montreal: McGill-Queen's University Press, 1996) 183–85. The New Connexionists were annexed by the Wesleyan Methodist Church in 1874. See Jennifer Grainger (ed.), *Delaware and Westminster Townships: Honouring Our Roots*, vol. I (London, ON: Westminster Township Historical Society, 2006), 246.

12. C.S. Baldwin, *Maple Grove and Beyond* (Ridgetown, ON: self-published, 2000), 48.

13. Kristine Nezezon and Louise Weston, *Bayham: Memories and Milestones* (Straffordville, ON: Municipality of Bayham, 2000) 53. Note that Hugh Sims calls him "Harry" in his *History of Elgin County*, vol. II, 72.

14. The Moravian sect originated in central Europe in Moravia and Bohemia in the fifteenth century. Officially the "Unity of the Brethren," this Protestant group migrated into Germany and eventually to the Americas in the eighteenth century. It was among the first to send Protestant missionaries into the New World. Its best known mission in southwestern Ontario was that of Fairfield on the Thames River. Established April 1792, the settlement consisted of six missionaries and 150 members of the Delaware First Nation. Destroyed by the Americans during the War of 1812, it was rebuilt on the south side of the Thames in 1815. Moraviantown, as it became known, was managed by Moravians until 1902, then transferred to the Methodists, and eventually taken over by the United Church of Canada. Perhaps the women in the story came from this mission. For more information, see Linda Sabathy-Judd (ed.), *Moravians in Upper Canada: The Diary of the Indian Mission of Fairfield on the Thames 1792–1813* (Toronto: Champlain Society, 1999).

15. The story is from Sims, *History*, vol. II, 72. He does not record the outcome.

16. The Templars at North Hall were probably a branch of the Independent Order of Good Templars, founded in Utica, New York, in 1851. Members of this lodge swore total abstinence from all intoxicating liquors. Now the International Order of Good Templars (IOGT), it still has lodges in many countries promoting non-use of alcohol and drugs and promoting peace and brotherhood. From www.templarhistory.com/goodtemplars.html, accessed February 16, 2008.

17. Corinth Women's Institute, *Tweedsmuir History*, vol. I.

18. Ibid.

19. Ross Andrews and Carol A. Judd, *Vienna: Historical Highlights from 1853 to 2003* (Straffordville: Municipality of Bayham, 2003), vi.

20. Richmond Women's Institute, *Tweedsmuir History*, vol. I.

Chapter Three: Township of Dunwich

1. Field, *Place Names*, 64.

2. Tyrconnell Women's Institute, *Tweedsmuir History*.

3. Sims, *History*, vol. I, 53.

4. Ella N. Lewis, *Sidelights on the Talbot Settlement* (St. Thomas, ON: Elgin Historical Society, 1938), 25.

5. Ibid., 26.

6. Ibid.

7. "Earthworks Preservation Dr. Coyne's Greatest Task," *St. Thomas Times-Journal*, September 1, 1930.

8. "Campbellton Had Its Own Post Office for Nearly Seventy Years," *Dutton Advance*, April 11, 1973.

9. W.F.H. Nicolaisen, *Scottish Place Names: Their Study and Significance* (London: B.T. Batsford, 1976), 52.

10. "Campbellton," April 11, 1973.

11. The Grange, an association of farmers, originated in Minnesota in 1867. The founder, Oliver Hudson Kelley, believed farmers needed a national organization to represent them, much as unions did industrial workers. He felt they were at the mercy of unscrupulous farm-supply merchants, railways, and warehouses. The Grange also championed education for rural areas and tried to improve country schools. Grange halls were community centres used for dances, potlucks, and political rallies. The organization continues to exist, primarily in the United States, representing the views of rural residents and the farming community. See www.grange.org, accessed February 18, 2008.

12. Performers at the 1951 event included two pipers from Ridgetown, the Paul Brothers and Shirley (character comedians), Margaret Lewis (who played an accordion), Mildred Moray (star of army shows), Joe Murphy (comedy impersonator), Dorothy Steadman (dancer and acrobat), the Shedden Male Quartet, and Billy Meek (who performed original songs and musical numbers). Tom Hamilton was master of ceremonies, and Jack Ayre was pianist and musical director. Taken from *Dutton Advance*, July 26, 1951.

13. Norman McWilliam, *The Station at the River: A History of Duff Presbyterian Church, Largie, Ontario* (self-published, 1996), 11.

14. *Dutton Advance*, August 18, 1921. Miles never rebuilt his store but fixed up a small barn as a dwelling; he subsisted by working for local farmers as a labourer. As the years went by he is said to have become a well-known local bootlegger. His barn was a meeting place for drinkers during prohibition, and at night the road was often lined with their cars. Personal communication with Don Carroll, September 26, 2007.

15. Kelly and Thomas, *Postal History*, 37.

16. John Kenneth Galbraith says nearly everyone around Cowal was named McCallum! Galbraith, *Scotch*, 12.

17. H.R. Page & Co., *Illustrated Historical Atlas of the County of Elgin* (Owen Sound, ON: Richardson, Bond and Wright Offset Edition, 1972), vol. XI.

18. "United Church of Canada: Elgin Presbytery."

19. Marion Campbell and Yvonne McCallum (eds.), *Cowal May 5, 1925: Tweedsmuir History of Cowal Community* (Dutton, 1984) 208. The title includes the date the Cowal Women's Institute was organized.

20. Don Carroll, *History of Chalmers.* www.dunwich.truepath.com/chistory.htm, accessed June 20, 2007.

21. Neil R. Darroch designed St. Thomas City Hall as well as the St. Thomas Public Library that opened in 1906. See History/Library/St. Thomas Public Library browser: www.dunwich.truepath.com/chistory.htm, accessed February 21, 2008.

22. Colin A. McGugan (ed.), *The Early History of Dunwich Township 1790–1903* (Dutton, ON: West Elgin Genealogical and Historical Society, 2004), 257.

23. Ibid., 167.

24. For more information on Cashmere, see Grainger, *Vanished Villages of Middlesex*, 189–96.

25. Campbell and McCallum, *Cowal*, 267.

26. *Illustrated Historical Atlas*, XI.

27. Campbell and McCallum, *Cowal*, 196.

28. Ibid., 214.

29. Ibid., 14.

30. Ibid., 13.

31. Donald L. Carroll, "The Cowal Ghost," in *Memories of St. Thomas and Elgin* (St. Thomas, ON: Friends of St. Thomas Public Library, 1997), 226–29.

32. "Oil Is Keeping Village of Cowal on Elgin's Map," in Dunwich Township Scrapbook, p. 10, in the Local History Clipping File, St. Thomas Public Library.

33. "Township Chosen by Colonel Talbot as a Place to 'Roost,' " *St. Thomas Times-Journal*, October 11, 1950.

34. McGugan, *Early History*, 40.

35. "First Survey of Dunwich in 1797," *Dutton Advance*, June 28, 1967.

36. "William Coyne's Recollections," in George Thorman (ed.), *Essays on Elgin County* (St. Thomas, ON: Elgin Historical Society, 1989), 22–23.

37. *Illustrated Historical Atlas*, XI.

38. John A. Patton, "Dunwich S.S. No. 3," in *A Pioneer History: Elgin Co.: Prize-Winning School Essays Published by James S. Brierley in the Southern Counties Journal* (St. Thomas, ON: 1896), 62.

39. Sims, *History*, vol. III, 191.

40. Patton, "Dunwich S.S. No. 3," 61.

41. Wallacetown Women's Institute, Tweedsmuir History, vol. I.

42. "The Dunwich Settlement and the Coyne Family," in George Thorman (ed.), *Essays on Elgin County*, 130.

43. Wallacetown Women's Institute, Tweedsmuir History, vol. I.

44. Patton, "Dunwich S.S. No. 3," 61.

45. Wallacetown Women's Institute, Tweedsmuir History, vol. I.

46. "Blast from the Past," *Dutton-Dunwich Horizon*, January 2007.

47. Wallacetown Women's Institute, Tweedsmuir History, vol. II.

48. Alan McMillan, "The Largie Community," a history project compiled for a class at West Elgin Secondary School, provided courtesy of Don Carroll.

49. "Mac," "Reminiscences of My School Days," *Dutton Advance*, April 11, 1889. This letter was supposed to be continued in later editions of the newspaper but was not because his Largie neighbours were annoyed by some of the tales he told! Personal communication with Don Carroll, September 26, 2007.

50. McWilliam, *Station*, 4.

51. The Largie Road was once Currie Road. Currie Road is now to the east. McGugan, *Early History*, 262–64.

52. McWilliam, *Station*, 2.

53. See Tait's Corners in Grainger, *Vanished Villages of Middlesex*, 91–93.

54. McGugan, *Early History*, 120.

55. In the Presbyterian church of the nineteenth century, the historical legacy of the Protestant Reformation of the sixteenth century still dominated thinking. For more information set in another Canadian context, see Richard Feltoe, *A Gentleman of Substance: The Life and Legacy of John Redpath (1796–1869)* (Toronto: Natural Heritage Books, 2004), 107.

56. Reverend Charles Gordon wrote *Glengarry School Days* and many other books under the pen name of Ralph Connor.

57. McWilliam, *Station*, 24.

58. J.K. Galbraith, "Legends and Ghost Stories of Early Days in Dunwich Township," *St. Thomas Times-Journal*, September 3, 1931.

59. The Patrons of Industry was an Ontario-based group modelled after the American Association of the Patrons of Industry founded in Michigan in 1889. Established in 1890, it was a farmers' organization that co-operated with the urban labour movement to address the political frustrations of both groups with big business. Its idea was to preserve the farming way of life against industrialization. It accomplished very little for farmers and was all but extinct by 1900. See www.trent.ca/admin/library/archives/91-1009.htm, accessed February 16, 2008.

60 McGugan, *Early History*, 121, 122.

61. Wallacetown Women's Institute, Tweedsmuir History, vol. II.

62. In later life Talbot jokingly confided to Anna Jameson that "Charlevoix … was, I believe, the true cause of my coming to this place. You know he calls this the 'Paradise of the Hurons.' Now I was

resolved to get to paradise by hook or by crook, and so I came here."
See Anna Brownell Jameson, *Winter Studies and Summer Rambles in
Canada* (Toronto: Thomas Nelson and Sons. Ltd., 1943) 112. Pierre
de Charlevoix was a French historian whose *Histoire et déscription
générale de la Nouvelle France* was the first general history of Canada.

63. Sims, *History*, vol. II, 175.

64. Lewis Burwell's original map of Colonel Talbot's farm is in Library
and Archives, Ottawa. Canada. It has been reprinted in many local
history books.

65. George Thorman, *Local History of Elgin County* (St. Thomas, ON:
self-published, 1965), 11–12.

66. Georgina Blackwood, "Dunwich S.S. No. 1," in *A Pioneer History*,
36.

67. Lewis, *Sidelights*, 24.

68. Thorman, *Local History*, 12.

69. Blackwood, "Dunwich S.S. No. 1," 36.

70. Sims, *History*, vol. II, 176.

71. Annie W. Geddes, "Tyrconnell S.S. No. 2," in *A Pioneer History*,
148.

72. John M. McLennan, "Dunwich S.S. No. 14," in *A Pioneer History*,
41.

73. Sims, *History*, vol. II, 176.

74. McGugan, *Early History*, 66.

75. Fred Coyne Hamil, *Lake Erie Baron: The Story of Colonel Thomas
Talbot.* (Toronto: Macmillan, 1955), 49.

76. Thorman, *Local History*, 13.

77. *Dutton Advance*, November 29, 1914.

78.   Edward Ermatinger, *Life of Colonel Talbot and the Talbot Settlement* (St. Thomas, ON: A. McLachlin's Home Journal Office, 1859), 100.

79.   Jameson, *Winter Studies and Summer Rambles*, 110–11.

80.   Thorman, *Local History*, 34.

81.   In Crimea, Richard Airey participated in one of wartime's best-known tragedies — the Charge of the Light Brigade. Lord Raglan dictated the order for the charge to Airey, who then passed it on to Nolan to be taken to the front. See W. Barring Pemberton, *Battles of the Crimean War* (London: B.T. Batsford, 1962) 91. New Glasgow, not far from Tyrconnell, was once known as Airey.

      Macbeth's London home, "Bleak House," is now the site of Lord Roberts Elementary School at 440 Princess Avenue. See Alice Gibb and Pat Morden, *Brackets and Bargeboards: Architectural Walks in London, Ontario* (Architectural Conservancy of Ontario, 1989), 53.

82.   Robin Winks, *The Blacks in Canada: A History* (Montreal: McGill University Press, 1971, reprint McGill-Queen's University Press, 1997), 78.

83.   Walter Pearce, "Dunwich S.S. No. 2," in *A Pioneer History*, 63.

84.   *Illustrated Historical Atlas*, XI.

85.   Colonel Richard Talbot (1630–91) became Earl and later Duke of Tyrconnell. One of his sisters, Frances, married Richard Talbot of Malahide, the branch of the family from which Colonel Thomas Talbot was descended. See *Burke's Dormant and Extinct Peerages* (Baltimore: Genealogical Publishing Co., 1985) 259. Tyrconnell is an English corruption of the Gaelic name for an area roughly corresponding to today's County Donegal. Personal communication, Roger Greene, Malahide Historical Society, September 16, 2007.

86.   Absalom Shade seems to have been an early entrepreneur in southwestern Upper Canada. He also acted as a land agent for William Dickson, a Niagara area merchant and politician. Dickson purchased a parcel of land in the township of Dumfries, on which Shade had built a sawmill and a gristmill. The community that developed around these facilities was originally called Shade's Mills but was renamed in honour of Dickson's friend John Galt, the first commissioner sent to

Upper Canada in 1826 by the Canada Company. The town of Galt is now part of Cambridge, Ontario.

87.   Black salts are crude potash or potassium carbonate, usually from wood ashes. Pearl ash is a more refined potash, created by baking potash in a kiln to remove impurities. The result is a fine white powder used in agriculture and in industry to make soap and glass.

88.   "William Coyne's Recollections," in *Essays*, 23.

89.   *Illustrated Historical Atlas*, XI.

90.   See Grainger, *Vanished Villages of Middlesex*, 189.

91.   Wallacetown Women's Institute, Tweedsmuir History, vol. I.

92.   Blackwood, "Dunwich S.S. No. 1," 35.

93.   Ibid.

94.   Tyrconnell Women's Institute, Tweedsmuir History.

95.   Pearce, "Dunwich S.S. No. 2," 67.

96.   McGugan, *Early History*, 245. No other source seems to mention an 1856 school.

97.   Provincial plaque in front of the church. The reference is to Randolph, 9th Earl of Galloway (1800–73), who was MP for Cockermouth (1826–31) and lord lieutenant of County Kirkcudbright (1828–45) and of County Wigtown (1828–51). See Charles Kidd and David Williamson (eds.), *Debrett's Illustrated Peerage* (London: Debrett's Peerage Ltd, 2000) 657. Being Irish, Galloway was probably an old crony of Colonel Talbot's.

98.   From plaque in front of church.

99.   Meredith Conn, Sr., *Journal of Meredith Conn Sr.* (1858) 22. The Millerite movement, founded in Upper Canada in various places in the 1840s, predicted the exact date when Christ would return. Its founder was William Miller. For more information, see Fred Landon, *Western Ontario and the American Frontier* (New York: Russell and Russell, 1970), 125.

100. Tyrconnell Women's Institute, Tweedsmuir History.

101. Sims, *History*, vol. III, 141.

102. W.C. Miller, "Early Industries in St. Thomas," in *Vignettes of Early St. Thomas* (St. Thomas, ON: Sutherland Press, 1967), 179.

103. "William Coyne's Recollections," in *Essays*, 23. Buller is sometimes referred to as "Bullen."

104. *Illustrated Historical Atlas*, XI.

105. *Armstrong & Co.'s County of Elgin Gazetteer and Directory 1872* (Armstrong & Co., 1872), 181.

106. *Illustrated Historical Atlas*, XI.

107. Tyrconnell Women's Institute, Tweedsmuir History.

108. McGugan, *Early History*, 134.

109. Ibid., 185.

110. *Dutton Advance*, July 7, 1892.

111. Pearce, "Dunwich S.S. No. 2," 66.

112. Arthur S. Godwin, "Tyrconnell District Oil Field Link with Pioneer of WO," *London Free Press*, July 11, 1950.

113. Hugh J. Sims, *Ghosts of Elgin's Past* (St. Thomas, ON: 1980), 103.

114. Wallacetown Women's Institute, Tweedsmuir History, vol. II.

115. Tyrconnell Women's Institute, Tweedsmuir History.

Chapter Four: Township of Malahide

1. Adrian Room, *A Dictionary of Irish Place Names* (Belfast: Appletree Press, 1986), 88.

2.   Stanley J. Stephens, *Port Bruce As I Have Known It: An Illustrated History* (self-published, 1975), 4.

3.   Levi Young, *Old Port Bruce: Letters* (1933).

4.   J.J. Talman, "Noble Catfish Creek Henry Dalley's Choice for Port Development," in Port Bruce Scrapbook, p. 1, in the Local History Clipping File, St. Thomas Public Library.

5.   J.J. Talman, "Launching Port Bruce Occasion for Oratory and Cheerful Outlook," in ibid.

6.   *Illustrated Historical Atlas*, VIII.

7.   Ella N. Lewis, *East Elgin Place Names* (St. Thomas, ON: Elgin Historical Society, 1935), 13.

8.   Stephens, *Port Bruce*, 35. For more information about this general, see Christopher Sykes, *Orde Wingate* (London: Collins, 1959).

9.   Although the house may have been named for its "dazzling whiteness" (Lewis, *East Elgin*, 11), according to one local historian, the Lewis family originated in Whitehall, New York (Sims, *Ghosts*, 33).

10.   Room, *Dictionary*, 50.

11.   Carter, *Place Names*, 839.

12.   "United Church of Canada: Elgin Presbytery."

13.   See www.gwcleminshaw.com/dunboyne.cfm, accessed February 16, 2008.

14.   Sims, *History*, vol. I, 113.

15.   See www.caasco.com, accessed June 21, 2007.

16.   Karen Bailey (ed.), *The Haggan Papers*, vol. IVa (Elgin County Library Board, 1979), 9.

17.   Ibid., 11. Reverend Edward Hartley Dewart, DD (1828–1903), was born in County Cavan, Ireland, in 1828 and came to Canada in 1834. A Methodist minister, he was editor of the *Christian Guardian*

1869–95. See C.C. James, *Canadian Poetry: A Bibliography* (Toronto: William Briggs, 1899), 18.

18. Ibid., 1–2. Wrong's specialty was Canadian and American history. Known as the "Dean of Canadian Historians," his books included *The Fall of Canada, Conquest of New France*, and *The Canadians*. He married Sophia Hume Blake, daughter of Edward Blake (1833–1912), second premier of Ontario (1871–72) and later leader of the federal Liberal party. Two sons died in the Great War, and son Hume Wrong (1894–1954) was ambassador to the United States (1945).

19. Horatio Nelson Chute, see www.famousamericans.net/horationelsonchute, accessed June 28, 2005.

20. Bailey, *Haggan Papers*, vol. IVa, 10. Peacock made music a major part of his teaching program, setting even geography, history, and multiplication tables to music. He introduced a school song:

> Clap, clap all together
> Clap, clap away.
> For Peacock's School is a happy place
> Upon a rainy day.

Some parents were apparently dissatisfied with his disciplinary methods, and he was replaced as teacher. After he began holding classes in the church, there was rivalry between the two village schools, and children are said to have had snowball fights during recess in winter.

21. Hume, *Capsule History*, 8.

22. *Aylmer Express*, June 2, 1892, 3.

23. Paul Brackenbury, "Robbery at Grovesend," in *Memories of St. Thomas and Elgin*, vol. I (St. Thomas, ON: Friends of St. Thomas Public Library, 1997), 66–68.

24. The story of the Marshall Piggott case comes from the following sources:
   Paul Brackenbury, "A Grovesend Murder: The Smith-Piggott Case," in *Memories*, 58–60; Sims, *History*, vol. I, 216–17; James S. Brierley, "1881 and Onward: Reminiscences of St. Thomas and Elgin County Half a Century Ago," reprinted from the *St. Thomas*

Times-Journal in 1931, 28–30; and GASLIGHT electronic text and discussion site, www.gaslight.mtroyal.ab.ca, accessed March 9, 2005. For more information on John Wilson Murray, Ontario's first full-time paid criminal detective, see Bruce McDougall, *John Wilson Murray* (Don Mills, ON: Fitzhenry & Whiteside, 1980).

25.   Sims, *History*, vol. I, 219.

26.   Jim Doelman, "Elgin County Public Schools," produced by the Elgin County Board of Education in 1982.

27.   Sims, *History*, vol. II, 250.

28.   Their cemetery is on the east side of Carter Road, north of Lakeview.

29.   Church information is from *Talbot Times*, 1, no. 4 (December 1982), 1 and 2, and www.elginogs.ca/cemeteries/malahide/lakeview.htm, accessed June 29, 2007.

30.   Information on these and other shipwrecks may be found at the following web sites:
        Maritime History of the Great Lakes: Shipwrecks: ERIE WAVE, www.hhpl.on.ca/GreatLakes/wrecks/Details.asp?ID=21864n=2, accessed July 10, 2005.
        Maritime History of the Great Lakes: Shipwrecks: ERIE WAVE, www.halinet.on.ca/GreatLakes/Documents/ (this site has changed since 2005, and the page no longer exists).
        Maritime Images of the Great Lakes: Images Search Results, www.hhpl.on.ca/greatlakes/glimages/results.sp?q=northern+indiana &st=KW. accessed July 10, 2005.

31.   *Aylmer Express*, July 7 1892, 4.

32.   Carter, *Place Names*, 38.

33.   Born in Norfolk County in the 1860s, John Henry Sharp had blacksmith shops in many localities. He died in St. Thomas on February 25, 1946. Sims, *History*, vol. I, 250. His obituary in the *St. Thomas Times-Journal* on February 28 states that his "reputation as an expert horseshoer brought him business from a wide area. Many owners of trotting horses took their steeds to Mr. Sharp."

34. Sims, *History*, vol. I, 250.

35. Ibid., vol. III, 16–17.

36. Doelman, "Elgin County Public Schools."

37. William D. Clutton, "Genealogy and Family History of William Clutton of Fressingfield, Suffolk, England and His Descendants," a manuscript in the personal collection of the author, 169.

Chapter Five: Township of South Dorchester

1. Armstrong, *Origin and Meaning*, 84.

2. Kingsmill-Mapleton Women's Institute, Tweedsmuir History, book 1.

3. Ibid.

4. Ibid.

5. *Churches of North Yarmouth and District* (North Yarmouth and District Historical Association, 1995), 13.

6. Ibid.

7. Kingsmill-Mapleton Women's Institute, Tweedsmuir History, book 1.

8. Sims, *History*, vol. II, 8.

9. *Churches of North Yarmouth*, 11.

10. James L. McCallum, *Stories of South Dorchester* (Ontario Genealogical Society Elgin County Branch, 1998), 26.

11. Kingsmill-Mapleton Women's Institute, Tweedsmuir History, book 1.

12. Ibid.

13. These are the names of the postmasters according to official records. Often the postmaster and storekeeper were one and the same, as we see in the similarity of names in the two lists. There is B. Knight,

who is probably Benjamin, and P.N. Boughner, who is likely Phillip. Thomas McKee appears on both lists, and Maud Bray is one of the Bray sisters. In the case of William A. Barrows, his name may have really been Baron, or vice versa!

14. *Armstrong and Co.'s County of Elgin Gazetteer and Directory for 1872* (Armstrong & Company, 1872), 164.

15. Kingsmill-Mapleton Women's Institute, Tweedsmuir History, book 1.

16. *Scarborough's Survey of Middlesex and Elgin Counties, Ontario* (Hamilton: Scarborough Company, 1910).

Chapter Six: Township of Southwold

1. Field, *Place Names*, 162.

2. Sims, *History*, vol. I, 50. The RCAF Bombing and Gunnery School (B&GS) was a unit of the British Commonwealth Air Training Plan. No. 4 B&GS had its main base at Fingal. It operated from November 25, 1940, to February 17, 1945, during which time it graduated over 6,000 non-pilot aircrew members. Many students lost their lives while training there. See the plaque at Fingal Wildlife Management Area on Fingal Road for their names and more information. The plaque does not say, however, whether the bombs frightened away ghosts.

3. Fife and McKillop, *Historical Sketches of Southwold Township School Sections*.

4. Story from www.elginogs.ca/cemeteries/southwold/hunter.htm, accessed June 19, 2007.

5. Balm of Gilead is a healing compound or balm made from the resinous gum of the poplar tree, traditionally used to produce cough syrup. It takes its name from the balm carried from Gilead by the caravan of merchants to whom Joseph was sold by his brothers; Genesis 37:25. See *New Encyclopedia Britannica*, vol. V (Chicago: Encyclopedia Britannica, 2007), 266.

6. This story is from "Boxall Named for Pioneers," in the Southwold Scrapbook 1, p. 9, in the Local History Clipping File, St. Thomas Public Library.

7.   The name is sometimes spelled "Smoke" or "Smuck."

8.   Sims, *History*, vol. XI, 11.

9.   Middlemarch Women's Institute, Tweedsmuir History.

10.   Ibid., 125.

11.   Rosa Hendershott, "S.S. No. 14 Southwold," in *A Pioneer History*, 30. Note, however, that Mr. Robinson may have thought the book by George Eliot was appropriate, since George Elliot Casey was Liberal MP for Elgin at the time and Mr. Robinson was one of his admirers. It has also been said that Robinson's daughter Hattie helped choose the name (Middlemarch Women's Institute, Tweedsmuir History, 5, 124). Casey ran for Parliament when only twenty-one. Being intelligent, well-educated, and charming, he was easily elected. He and his wife "immediately shone brightly in the society of the Capital." However, he is said not to have lived up to his promise. (Brierley, *1881*, 20).

12.   Middlemarch Women's Institute, Tweedsmuir History, 125.

13.   Ibid.

14.   Ibid., 110

15.   The Bible Christians were one of the branches of the Methodist church. They joined other Methodists in 1884 to form the Methodist Church of Canada. See Grainger (ed.), *Delaware and Westminster*, 246.

16.   Middlemarch Women's Institute, Tweedsmuir History, 30.

17.   "United Church of Canada: Elgin Presbytery."

18.   Middlemarch Women's Institute, Tweedsmuir History, 46.

19.   Ibid.

20.   Maggie McLennan, "S.S. No. 11," in *A Pioneer History*, 119–22.

21.   Fife and McKillop, "Historical Sketches of Southwold Township School Sections."

22.   Sims, *History*, vol. I, 58.

23. Wallacetown Women's Institute, Tweedsmuir History, vol. I.

24. McLennan, "S.S. No. 11," 122.

25. Ibid.

26. The author believes this is the same Crowell Wilson (1815–94) who went on to become prominent in London Township. He was in the milling business as early as 1839, west of the Proof Line (now Richmond Street). His carding mill operated into the early 1860s. He retained his interest in education, however, becoming superintendent of London Township schools in 1844. He entered politics in 1851 and was elected to the parliament of the Province of Canada representing the London District (Middlesex and Elgin). He is buried at Arva Cemetery, where his tombstone reads, "A member of the Canadian Parliament at the time of Confederation." See *London Township: A Rich Heritage 1796–1997*, vol. I (Arva, ON: London Township History Book Committee, 2001).

27. Dictionary of Canadian Biography Online. www.biographi.ca/EN/ShowBio.asp?BioId=39435, accessed July 6, 2007.

28. McLennan, "S.S. No. 11," 123.

29. Ibid., 118.

30. Sims, *History*, vol. I, 59.

31. Fife and McKillop, "Historical Sketches of Southwold Township School Sections."

32. Sims, *History*, vol. III, 218.

33. Kelly and Thomas, *Postal History*, 56.

34. Matthew 15:39 refers to Magdala.

Chapter Seven: Township of Yarmouth

1. Sims, *History*, vol. I, 6. An amusing story is associated with this railway stop. On one occasion a man named Alfred Bucke was waiting in the doorway of the tiny station, in which about thirty people were

sheltering from the cold and rain. As the train approached, Bucke spotted a friend on the nearby road and waved his umbrella to him in greeting. The train engineer took the man's wave as a signal to keep going and acknowledged it with a toot from his whistle. Bucke was left to face the irate would-be passengers who had been planning a day's shopping in St. Thomas. The date of the story is unknown, but Bucke died in 1957, aged ninety-three. See Yarmouth Glen Women's Institute, Tweedsmuir History.

2.   Sims, *History*, vol. I, 46–47.

3.   Butler's Rangers was a Loyalist regiment fighting for the British during the American Revolution. Formed by John Butler, the unit was raised in 1777. A key factor in its success was its close co-operation with various Aboriginal nations with which it served and its extensive use of guerrilla tactics. It fought in what are now the states of New York, Pennsylvania, Ohio, Virginia, Kentucky, and Michigan. After the revolution, they returned to the Niagara area. Most received land grants in Upper Canada as United Empire Loyalists. See www.iaw.on.ca/~awoolley/brang/brang/html, accessed February 16, 2008.

4.   Louisa V. Prior, "Yarmouth," *A Pioneer History*, 164.

5.   *S. S. # 4 Barnum's Gully*, booklet at Port Stanley Public Library.

6.   Sims, *History*, vol. I, 107.

7.   "Lived over Sixty Years on One Farm in Yarmouth," a typewritten copy of a *St. Thomas Times* article from 1912, at Elgin County Archives.

8.   Ibid.

9.   *C.F. Fuller's Counties of Elgin and Norfolk Directory for 1865 and 1866* (Blackburn's City Steam Press, 1866), 80.

10.   South Yarmouth Women's Institute, Tweedsmuir History, vol. III.

11.   Directories continue for years to mention a Dexter General Store but may have been using out-of-date information. The store is not standing today.

12.   Sims, *Ghosts*, 20.

13. *Smith's Canadian Gazetteer, 1846* (Coles Publishing Company, 1970), 88.

14. Stephens, *Port Bruce*, 47.

15. Ella H. Martyn, "Yarmouth," in *A Pioneer History*, 162.

16. Famous fights — boxing history. www.famous-fights.com/search?updated-max=2007=07-1-T20%A00%2B01%3A00&max-results=8, accessed June 15, 2007.

17. "Boxing News," www.boxingscene.com/?m=show&id=3098, accessed June 15, 2007.

18. Bob Mee, *Bare Fists: The History of Bare-Knuckle Prize-Fighting* (Woodstock, NY: Overlook Press, 2001), 118.

19. Sims, *Ghosts*, 23.

20. Ibid.

21. Young, *Old Port Bruce*.

22. Brian Masschaele (ed.), *Tremaine's Map of the County of Elgin, 1864: Commemorative Edition in Celebration of the Sesquicentennial of the County of Elgin, 1852–2002* (St. Thomas, ON: Elgin County Library, 2002), 26.

23. Martyn, "Yarmouth," 162.

24. *Illustrated Historical Atlas*, vol. X.

25. Martyn, "Yarmouth," 162.

26. Ibid.

27. Sims, *History*, vol. I, 238.

28. Sims, *Ghosts*, 25A.

29. Ibid., 37.

30. *Illustrated Historical Atlas*, 40.

31. Paddon, *Glimpses*, 100.

32. Miller, "The Market Controversy," in *Vignettes*, 215.

33. Brierley, *1881 and Onwards*, 14, 15.

34. From www.execulink.com/~firby/history.html#Firbys (web site of Arnold R. Firby of St. Thomas), accessed October 4, 2007.

35. "United Church of Canada: Elgin Presbytery."

36. Miller, "The Market Controversy," in *Vignettes*, 215.

37. Sims, *History*, vol. II, 80, calls him "Selbenky." The same author in *Ghosts*, 39, calls him "Selberky." The "Sebisky" variant comes from Versa Gloin, "S.S. No. 13 Yarmouth," in *A Pioneer History*, 171.

38. Sims, *History*, vol. II, 80.

39. This assertion is found in Lewis, *East Elgin*, 21. However, there was no Lord Selborne until 1872, according to *Debrett's Peerage and Baronetage* (London: Debrett's Peerage, 1980), 1056.

40. Selborne, Hampshire, is best known as the setting for *The Natural History of Selborne in the County of Southampton*, written by nineteenth-century naturalist Gilbert White.

41. Frank and Nancy Prothero, *Port Stanley: Musings and Memories* (Port Stanley: Nan-Sea Publications, 1980), 123.

42. Thorman, *Local History*, 49.

43. *Smith's Canadian Gazetteer 1846*, 167.

44. Sims, *History*, vol. II, 157.

45. Christopher Smith, *The Mill from Selbourne* (1995), 6.

46. John Widdifield is also referred to as "Henry."

47. Union and Area Women's Institute, Tweedsmuir History, 131.

48. South Yarmouth Women's Institute, Tweedsmuir History, vol. III.

49.   Union and Area Women's Institute, Tweedsmuir History, 129.

50.   Sims, *History*, vol. III, 220.

Selected Bibliography

Historic Atlases, Directories, Maps, and Gazetteers

Armstrong & Co.'s County of Elgin Gazetteer and Directory 1872. Armstrong & Co., 1872.

C. F. Fuller's Counties of Elgin and Norfolk Directory for 1865 & 1866. Blackburn's City Steam Press, 1866.

Illustrated Historical Atlas of the County of Elgin. Toronto: H.R. Page & Co., 1877.

Masschaele, Brian (ed.), *Tremaine's Map of the County of Elgin, 1864: Commemorative Edition in Celebration of the Sesquicentennial of the County of Elgin, 1852–2002.* St. Thomas, ON: Elgin County Library, 2002.

Scarborough's Survey of Middlesex and Elgin Counties, Ontario. Hamilton, ON: Scarborough Company, 1910.

Smith's Canadian Gazetteer, 1846. Toronto: Coles Publishing Company, 1970. Originally published by William Wye Smith in 1846.

Selected References

Andrews, Ross, and Carol A. Judd, *Vienna: Historical Highlights from 1853 to 2003.* Straffordville, ON: Municipality of Bayham, 2003.

Armstrong, G.H., *The Origin and Meaning of Place Names in Canada.* Toronto: Macmillan, 1930.

Bailey, Karen (ed.), *The Haggan Papers.* Elgin County Library Board, 1979.

Baldwin, C.S., *Maple Grove and Beyond.* Ridgetown, ON: self-published, 2000.

Baldwin, Paul, "Cycle Historic Elgin: With Local History Essays and Suggested Route," self-published pamphlet, n.d.

Barons, Kirk, "Pioneer Churches and a Brief History of Bayham Township," pamphlet, 1977, in the London Public Library.

Brierley, James S., *1881 and Onward: Reminiscences of St. Thomas and Elgin County Half a Century Ago*. St. Thomas, ON: 1931.

_____, *A Pioneer History: Elgin County: Prize-winning School Essays Published by James S. Brierley in the Southern Counties Journal*. St. Thomas, ON: 1896.

Brown, Ron, *Ghost Railways of Ontario*. Toronto: Polar Bear Press, 1998.

Burke's Dormant and Extinct Peerages. Baltimore: Genealogical Publishing Co., 1985.

Cameron, Kenneth, *English Place Names*. London: B.T. Batsford, 1977.

Campbell, Marion, and Yvonne McCallum (eds.), *Cowal May 5, 1925: Tweedsmuir History of Cowal Community*. Dutton, ON: self-published, 1984.

Carroll, Don, *History of Chalmers*. www.dunwich.truepath.com/chistory.htm, accessed June 20, 2007.

Carter, Floreen, *Ghost Post Offices of Ontario*. Oakville, ON: Personal Impressions, 1986.

_____, *Place Names of Ontario*. London, ON: Phelps Publishing, 1985.

"Churches of North Yarmouth and District," pamphlet produced by the North Yarmouth and District Historical Association in 1995, in the Belmont Public Library.

Clutton, William D., "Genealogy and Family History of William Clutton of Fressingfield, Suffolk, England, and His Descendants," booklet in the personal collection of the author.

Coleman, Thelma, *The Canada Company*. Stratford, ON: County of Perth and Cumming Publishers, 1978.

Corinth Women's Institute, Tweedsmuir History. www.elgin.ca/tweedsmuir/bayham.html

Crinan Women's Institute, Tweedsmuir History. www.elgin.ca/tweedsmuir/aldborough.html

Debrett's Peerage and Baronetage. London: Debrett's Peerage, 1980.

Doelman, Jim, *Elgin County Public Schools*. Elgin County Board of Education, 1982.

Elgin County: An Introduction. Research Report No. 1, Elgin County Local Government Study, 1975.

Ermatinger, Edward, *Life of Colonel Talbot and the Talbot Settlement*. St. Thomas, ON: A. McLachlin's Home Journal Office, 1859.

Field, John, *Place Names of Great Britain and Ireland*. Newton Abbott, England: David and Charles, 1980.

Fife, G., and Elsye A.R. McKillop (eds.), "Historical Sketches of Southwold Township School Sections, 1971," pamphlet in the London Room, Central Public Library, London.

Galbraith, John Kenneth, *The Scotch*. Toronto: Macmillan of Canada, 1964.

George, E.B., *Vignettes of the Old Pere Marquette in Canada*. London, ON: F.J. Ram, 1990.

Gibb, Alice (ed.), *London Township: A Rich Heritage 1796–1997*. Vol. I. Arva, ON: London Township History Book Committee, 2001.

Gibb, Alice, and Pat Morden, *Brackets and Bargeboards: Architectural Walks in London, Ontario*. Architectural Conservancy of Ontario, 1989.

Grainger, Jennifer, *Vanished Villages of Middlesex*. Toronto: Natural Heritage Books, 2002.

Grainger, Jenny (ed.), *Delaware and Wesrminister Townships: Honouring Our Roots*. Vol. I. London, ON: Westminister Township Historical Society, 2006.

Hamil, Fred Coyne, *Lake Erie Baron: The Story of Colonel Thomas Talbot*. Toronto: Macmillan, 1955.

Hume, Giles A., *A Capsule History of East Elgin*. St. Thomas, ON: Elgin County Library Board, 1975.

James, C.C., *Canadian Poetry: A Bibliography*. Toronto: William Briggs, 1899.

Jameson, Anna Brownell, *Winter Studies and Summer Rambles in Canada*. Toronto: Thomas Nelson and Sons Ltd, 1943, reprint.

Johnston, Wilfred C., *Catholic Churches of West Elgin: More Than a Century of Christian Service*. London: Diocese of London, 1979.

Kelly, Keith, and Irving Thomas, *A Postal History of West Elgin*. West Elgin Historical and Genealogical Society, 1999.

Kidd, Charles, and David Williamson (eds.), *Debrett's Illustrated Peerage*. London: Debrett's Peerage Ltd, 2000.

Kingsmill-Mapleton Women's Institute, Tweedsmuir History, at George Thorman Room, St. Thomas Public Library.

Landon, Fred, *Western Ontario and the American Frontier*. New York: Russell and Russell, 1970.

Lashbrook, Harley, *Aldborough: The Township with a Past*. West Lorne, ON: Webco Publications, 2001.

Lashbrook, Nancy, *West Lorne: 90 Years a Village*. West Lorne, ON: Webco Publications, 1997.

Lee, Robert C., *The Canada Company and the Huron Tract 1826-1853*. Toronto: Natural Heritage, 2004.

Lewis, Ella N., *East Elgin Place Names*. St. Thomas, ON: Elgin Historical Society, 1935.

_____, *Sidelines on the Talbot Settlement*. St. Thomas, ON: Elgin Historical Society, 1938.

MacIntyre, J.H. (ed.), *The Pioneer Days in Aldborough*. Aldborough Old Boys Association, 1933.

McCallum, James L., *Stories of South Dorchester*. Ontario Genealogical Society Elgin County Branch, 1998.

McDougall, Bruce, *John Wilson Murray*. Don Mills: Fitzhenry & Whiteside, 1980.

McGugan, Colin A. (ed.), *The Early History of Dunwich Township 1790–1903*. Dutton, ON: West Elgin Genealogical and Historical Society, 2004.

McMillan, Alan, "The Largie Community," history project for West Elgin Secondary School, courtesy of Donald Carroll.

McWilliam, Norman, *The Station at the River: A History of Duff Presbyterian Church, Largie, Ontario*. Largie, ON: self-published, 1996.

Mee, Bob, *Bare Fists: The History of Bare-Knuckle Prize-Fighting*. Woodstock, NY: Overlook Press, 2001.

Memories of St. Thomas and Elgin. St. Thomas, ON: Friends of St. Thomas Public Library, 1997.

Middlemarch Women's Institute, Tweedsmuir History, at Archives and Research Collections Centre, University of Western Ontario.

Miller, W.C., *Vignettes of Early St. Thomas*. St. Thomas, ON: Sutherland Press, 1967.

New Encyclopedia Britannica. Vol. V. Chicago: Encyclopedia Britannica, 2007.

Nezezon, Kristine, and Louise Weston, *Bayham: Memories and Milestones*. Straffordville, ON: Municipality of Bayham, 2000.

Paddon, Wayne, *Glimpses into St. Thomas Railway: The Canada Southern Railway*. Vol. I. Paddon Books, 1989.

_____, *"Steam and Petticoats" 1840–1890: The Early Railway Era in Southwestern Ontario*. Paddon Books, 1977.

Pemberton, W. Barring, *Battles of the Crimean War*. London: B.T. Batsford, 1962.

Prothero, Frank, and Prothero, Nancy, *Port Stanley: Musings and Memories*. Port Stanley, ON: Nan-Sea Publications, 1980.

Rayburn, Alan, *Place Names of Ontario*. Toronto: University of Toronto Press, 1997.

Richmond Women's Institute, Tweedsmuir History, at Bayham Public Library.

Room, Adrian, *A Dictionary of Irish Place Names*. Belfast: Appletree Press, 1986.

"S.S. # 4 Barnum's Gully," booklet at Port Stanley Public Library.

Sabathy-Judd, Linda (ed.), *Moravians in Upper Canada: The Diary of the Indian Mission of Fairfield on the Thames 1792—1813*. Toronto: Champlain Society, 1999.

Semple, Neil, *The Lord's Dominion: The History of Canadian Methodism*. Montreal: McGill-Queen's University Press, 1996.

Sims, Hugh J., *Ghosts of Elgin's Past*. St. Thomas, ON: self-published, 1980.

———, *Sims' History of Elgin County*. St. Thomas, ON: Elgin County Library, 1984.

Smith, Douglas N.W., *The New York Central in Canada: Southern Ontario Lines*. Vol. I. Ottawa: Trackside Canada, 1998.

Smith, John Christopher, *The Mill from Selborne*. Aylmer, ON: Aylmer Express, 1995.

South Yarmouth Women's Institute, Tweedsmuir History. www.elgin.ca/tweedsmuir/yarmouth.html

Stephens, Stanley J., "Port Bruce As I Have Known It: An Illustrated History," pamphlet dated 1975, at London Room, Central Public Library, London.

Thorman, George, *Local History of Elgin County*. St. Thomas, ON: self-published, 1965.

Thorman, George (ed.), *Essays on Elgin County*. St. Thomas, ON: Elgin Historical Society, 1989.

Township of Yarmouth Centennial. Yarmouth Township, 1967.

Tyrconnell Women's Institute, Tweedsmuir History. www.elgin.ca/tweedsmuir/dunwich.html

"United Church of Canada: Elgin Presbytery," photocopy of typescript at London Room, Central Public Library, London.

Wallacetown Women's Institute, Tweedsmuir History. www.elgin.ca/tweedsmuir/dunwich.html

West Lorne Women's Institute, Tweedsmuir History, photocopy of a typescript at London Room, Central Public Library, London.

Winks, Robin, *Blacks in Canada: A History*. Montreal: McGill University Press, 1971, reprint McGill-Queen's University Press, 1997.

Yarmouth Glen Women's Institute, Tweedsmuir History. www.elgin.ca/tweedsmuir/yarmouth.html

Young, Levi, "Old Port Bruce: Letters," an unpublished manuscript, dated 1933, in the Central Public Library, London.

Web Sites

Boxing News. www.boxingscene.com/?m=show&id=3098, accessed June 15, 2007.

CAA South Central Ontario. www.caasco.com, accessed June 21, 2007.

Cleminshaw Home Page. www.gwcleminshaw.com/dunboyne.cfm, accessed February 21, 2008.

Dictionary of Canadian Biography Online, www.biographi.ca/EN/ShowBio.asp?BioId=39435query=james%20AND%20Watson, accessed July 6, 2007.

Famous Fights – boxing history. www.famous-fights.com/search?updated-max=2007=07-10T20%3A00%2B01%3A00&max-results=8, accessed June 15, 2007.

Firby Cemetery, Bayham Township, Elgin County, Ontario. www.elginogs.ca/cemeteries/bayham/firby.htm, accessed June 25, 2007.

GASLIGHT electronic text and discussion site. gaslight.mtroyal.ab.ca, accessed March 9, 2005.

Hamlets Villages and Towns. www.elginconnects.ca/portal/entry.php?w=EdisonMuseumHamletsVillagesandTowns&e_id=240, accessed December 15, 2007.

History/Library/St. Thomas Public Library browse. www.st=thomas.library.on.ca/index.php/Library/History, accessed February 21, 2008.

Home Page of Arnold Firby, St. Thomas, Ontario. www.execulink.com/~firby/history.html, accessed October 4, 2007.

Horatio Nelson Chute. famousamericans.net/horationelsonchute, accessed June 28, 2005.

Hunter Cemetery, Southwold Township, Elgin County, Ontario. www.elginogs.ca/cemeteries/southwold/hunter.htm, accessed June 19, 2007.

The Knights Templar: Independent Order of Good Templars. www.templarhistory.com/goodtemplars.html, accessed February 16, 2008.

Lakeview Cemetery, Malahide Township, Elgin County, Ontario. www.elginogs.ca/cemeteries/malahide/lakeview.htm, accessed June 29, 2007.

Local History, www.elginconnects.ca/portal/entry.php?w=BayhamLocalHistory&e_id=554, accessed December 15, 2007.

Maritime History of the Great Lakes: Shipwrecks: ERIE WAVE.www.halinet.on.ca/GreatLakes/Documents/, accessed July 10, 2005. The web site has changed since 2005, and that page no longer exists.

Maritime History of the Great Lakes: Shipwrecks: ERIE WAVE. www.hhpl.on.ca/ GreatLakes/wrecks/Details.asp?ID=21864&n=2, accessed July 10, 2005.

Maritime Images of the Great Lakes: Images Search Results www.hhpl.on.ca/greatLakes/glimages/results.asp?q=northern+indiana&st=KW, accessed July 10, 2005.

Patrons of Industry. www.trentu.ca/admin/library/archives/91-1009.htm, accessed February 18, 2008.

WWW.GRANGE.ORG – In Essentials, Unity – In Non-Essentials, Liberty – In All Things, Charity. www.grange.org, accessed February 18, 2008.

Index

Bowes, William (Maple Grove), 30

Boxall: 119–22

  brickyard, 122

  church, 121

  post office, 122

  school, 119, 121

Boxall, Harry (Boxall), 122

Bradfield, H. (Griffin's Corners), 28

Brantford (Brant County), 5

Brasher, George (McCurdy's
  Corners), 32

Bray, Maud (Mapleton), 115, 178

Bray sisters (Mapleton), 114

Breck's Bulbs (Lakeview), 105

Bridgeman, Ed (Mapleton), 116

British Commonwealth Air
  Training Program, 119

Brock, Isaac (Gen.), 69

Brock's Creek (Eagle), 3

Brodie, John (Mapleton), 116

Brodie, Sarah (Kintyre), 15

Brown, Henry (Crossley-Hunter),
  113

Brown, James F. (Mapleton), 116

Brown, John (Port Talbot), 70

Brown, Sebisky/Selbenky/Selberky
  (Pleasant Valley), 151

Brown, W. H. (Mapleton), 116

Bruce, James (Earl of Elgin) (Gov.
  Gen.), xii, 90

Bruce County, xii

Brydens (Crinan), 11

Buchanan, John (Campbellton), 45

Bucke, Alfred (Adrian), 180

Buller and Haynes (Tyrconnell),
  75, 80

Buffalo (NY), 4, 74, 78, 90, 142

Burdick, Caleb (Rev.) (Newell's
  Corners), 106

Burgess, Robert (Mapleton), 116

Burwell:

  Adam, 40

  Mahlon (Col.), 39–44, 66–68,
  70, 75, 130, 154

  Edward, 41

  Hercules, 77

  Lewis, 67, 170

  Sarah (Mrs. Adam), 40

  Sarah (Haun) (Mrs. Mahlon),
  40, 42, 44, 68

Burwell's Corners: 39–44, 70, 123,
  130

  cheese factory, 40, 42

  church, 42, 44

  founding of, 40

  registry office, 40, 41

Butler's Rangers, 137, 181

Calton (Malahide Township), 25,
  104

Cameron, Ewen (Watson's
  Corners), 130

Cameron, Peter (Tyrconnell), 75

Campbell, Archibald, Earl of
  Argyle, 45

Campbell, Archibald C. (Cowal), 50

Campbell, John (Cowal), 50

Campbell, Phil (Cowal), 54

Campbell, Robert (Campbellton), 45

Campbellton: 44–46, 63

  blacksmith shop, 45

  church, 45

  post office, 45, 46

  school, 45, 46

  general store, 45, 46

Campbeltown, see Campbellton

Campbeltown (Scotland), 45

Canada Company, 3, 4, 159, 172

Canada Southern Railway, 10, 16,
  18, 19, 149, 161, 162

Davis, ___ (Deacon) (Rogers Corners), 107
Davis, John (Malahide), 66, 106
Davis, Simeon (Rogers Corners), 107
Davis, Stephen (Port Bruce), 90
Dean, David (Maple Grove), 31
Delaware (Middlesex County), 67
Detroit (MI), 19, 64, 72, 83, 149
Devonport (Davenport: 87–92
 businesses, 89, 90
 resorts at, 92
Dewart, E. H., 174, 175
Dexter: 121, 139–41
 businesses, 140, 141
 churches, 140, 141
Dexter Community Hall, 141
Dickenson, W. E. (Long Point), 99
Digby County (Nova Scotia), 23
Doan, John (Mapleton), 114
Dobbie's Cemetery, 33
Doolittle, Ephraim H. (Lakeview), 104
Doolittle, Perry (Dunboyne), 94
Dorchester (Dorset, England), 109
Dorchester Township (Middlesex County), xii, 109
Drake, Keith (Mapleton), 116, 117
Dresden (Kent County), 56
Duart (Kent County), 5
Duff, Alexander (Sir), 59
Dufferin, Lord (Gov. Gen.), 93
Dunboyne: 92–94
 businesses, 93
 church, 93, 94
 post office, 93
 school, 93
Dunboyne Cheese and Butter Factory, 93
Dunwich (Suffolk, England), 39

Dunwich Oil Company, 82, 83
Dunwich Pier Company, 82
Dunwich, Township of, xii, xiv, 38–86
Durdle, James (Jamestown), 143
Dutton (Dunwich Township), 10, 11, 46, 49, 53, 57, 63
Dutton Advance, 14, 59, 70
Dutton-Dunwich, Municipality of, 39
Dyke, James, 98, 99

Eagle (Aldborough Township), 3, 15, 17
Earnshaw, ___ (Mr.) (Selbourne), 153
Eden (Bayham Township), 31
Edgar, Tom (North Hall), 34
Egner, Mr. and Mrs. Sebastian (Wiener's Corners), 158
Ekfrid Township (Middlesex County), 7, 47, 49, 63
Elgin (Morayshire, Scotland), xii
Elgin County Railroad Museum, 150
Elgin Historical Society (formerly Elgin County Historical and Scientific Society), 43, 44, 73, 84
Elgin Junior Institute, 53
Ellison, William (Middlemarch teacher), 125
Else, Leonard (Boxall), 122
England, 1, 87, 89, 109, 114, 119, 122, 131, 139, 143
Erb, Paul (Rev.), 6
Erie (PA), 74
Erie Wave (schooner), 103
Essex, County of, xii, 41
Estherville: 23–26
 church, 25

dance hall, 25, 26
shipyard, 23, 25
Exeter (England), 139

Farlane, John Miles (Tyrconnell), 77
Farlane, ___ (Mrs. J.M.)
    (Tyrconnell), 77
Fenian Raids, 82, 138
Ferndell (Aldborough Townhip), 14
Fillmore, Henry (Watson's
    Corners), 131
Fingal (Elgin County), 47, 122, 131,
    133, 153, 178
Fingal Bombing and Gunnery
    School, 119, 178
Fingal Wildlife Management Area,
    178
Firby: 26, 27, 94
    cemetery, 26, 27
    church, 26, 27
    mill, 27
Firby, Robert (Firby), 27
Firby, Thomas (Firby), 26, 27
Firby Cheese Factory, 27
First Middlesex Militia, 40
First World War (Great War), 19,
    53, 116
Fishback, Harvey (Mapleton), 116
Fisher, Benjamin (Dexter), 140
Fitch, ___ (Elder) (McCurdy's
    Corners), 32
Flannery, W. (Father), 4
Fleming, James (Kintyre), 15
Fletcher, Hugh (Cowal), 47
Floto, Dan (Firby), 27
Fonger, Ralph (Mapleton), 115
Foresters Lodge (Cowal) 51
Franklins (Grovesend), 98
Fraser, John (Maple Grove), 31
Fraser, Laura (Goodrich), 31

Fraser Valley, see Maple Grove
Free Church of Scotland, 59
Freeman, Charles "Canadian
    Giant," 142, 143, 148
Freeman, John (Rogers Corners),
    108
Froggett's Corners, see Griffin's
    Corners
Froggett, J.W. (Griffin's Corners),
    29
Fry, Ken (Mapleton), 116

G.N. Procunier and Sons, 37
Gaelic language, 8, 48, 60, 133
Galbraith, Donald (Largie), 59
Galbraith, Walter (Port Talbot), 67
Galloway, Earl of, 78
Garbutt, Henry (Rev.), 58
Gardiner:
    Anna, see Anna Coyne
    Singleton (Cashmere), 55, 76
    Thomas (Tyrconnell), 55, 76, 77
Geary, ___ (Mr.) (Middlemarch), 129
Germany, 1, 164
Gill, John (Campbellton), 45
Gilmore, Malcolm (Cowal), 51
Glencoe (Middlesex County), 11, 63
Glencolin: 95, 96
    businesses, 95, 96
    post office, 95, 96
    school, 95
Glen Erie (dance hall), see
    Estherville
Godby, G.H. (Griffin's Corners), 28
Godby, J. (Griffin's Corners), 28
Godfrey, W.E. (Grovesend), 97
Goodrich family (Maple Grove), 31
Goodrich, Laura, see Laura Fraser
Gordon, Charles W. (Rev.), 61, 169
Gordon, Mac, 64

McKee, Thomas (Mapleton), 114, 115

McKenzie, Earl (Mapleton), 114, 116

McKenzie, James (Cowal), 51

McKenzie, Peter (Cowal), 51

McKeracher, Mary (Campbellton), 45

McKeracher, ___ (Mr.) (Campbellton), 45

McKillop:
   Archibald (McKillop's Corners), 15
   Archibald, Jr. (McKillop's Corners), 15–17
   Duncan (West Lorne), 15–17, 45

McKillop, John (Tyrconnell), 82

McKillop, Neil (West Magdala), 133

McKillop's Corners (Aldborough Township), 15, 16, 19

MvKinnon, Neil (Rev.) (Crinan), 8

McLachlan, Alex (Cowal), 47

McLachlin, ___ (Mrs.) (Mapleton), 114

McLellan, John (Watson's Corners), 130

McMillan, Catherine (Brodie), 15

McMillan, Robert (Crinan), 10

McNabb, D. A. (Cowal), 51

McNabb, Peter (Cowal), 49

McNeil, Peter (Crinan), 9

McPhee, John, 7

McPherson, Allen (Largie), 61,62

McPherson, Daniel (Largie), 62

McPherson, Dave (Crinan), 11

McPherson, Hugh (Largie), 61

McPherson, Jane (Campbellton), 45

McPherson, Mary (Campbellton), 45

McRae, Donald (Largie), 61

McTavish:
   Christine (Cowal), 50
   John (Cowal), 49
   Nancy (Cowal), 49

McVey, John (Johnstown), 145

McVey, Margaret (Johnstown), 145

McWilliam, ___ (Mr.) (Largie), 62

McWilliam, Norman (Largie), 46

Meek, Billy (entertainer), 166

Meikle, James (Maple Leaf), 111

Melbourne (Middlesex County), 49

Mennonite, 96, 113

Merrill, Joseph (Estherville), 23, 25

Merrill's Corners, see Estherville, 23, 25

Methodists, 8, 16, 25, 30, 33, 34, 55, 58, 79, 93–95, 97, 106, 112, 113, 118, 120, 123, 127, 131, 137, 138, 140, 141, 164, 174, 179

Michigan Central Railroad, 19, 20, 124, 162

Mickleborough, J. & W., (St. Thomas), 150

Middlemarch: 124–29
   businesses, 124, 126
   church, 127–29
   organizations, 127
   post office, 125, 128
   school, 124, 125, 127
   station, 127, 128

Middlesex County, xii–xiv, 4, 7, 9, 10, 40, 41, 47, 48, 67, 76, 109, 148

Midgeley, John (St. Thomas),149

Mihell, Edward and Sarah (Devonport), 89

Mihell's Tailor Shop (Millersburg), 149

ABOUT THE AUTHOR

JENNIFER GRAINGER trained as an archaeologist at the Universities of Toronto and London, England, but local history has become her passion. *Vanished Villages of Elgin* is a companion study to her 2002 book, *Vanished Villages of Middlesex*. Jenny has also edited a two-volume history of Westminster and Delaware townships called *Honouring Our Roots*. She lives in London with her dog, Sandy, and hundreds of books.